"Brad has the amazing ability to bring together practical, applicable principles with thoughtful, people-focused counsel. I have never come away from a training with or reading by Brad where I have not learned something from him. Everything he writes is borne of experience, mistakes, and listening, and it builds on mission at the heart. I highly commend this book to you!"

Steve G. W. Moore, CEO and executive director of the M. J. Murdock Charitable Trust

"The believers in Philippi partnered with Paul's ministry through financial giving, and it is clear from Paul's thank-you letter that it arose from a deep and joy-filled friendship between them. That is the biblical principle that weaves through Brad Layland's book. Brad shows, simply and clearly, how to turn the assumption that funding for Christian ministry is fundamentally relational into practical plans and respectful encounters. It might have been titled *Turning Donors into Friends* (or vice versa). Speaking from working with The FOCUS Group, I can simply say on behalf of Langham Partnership, 'It works!'"

Christopher J. H. Wright, Langham Partnership, author of *The Shortfall: Owning the Challenge of Ministry Funding*

"I'm excited about Brad Layland's new book *Turning Donors into Partners*, as it is timely for serious fundraising professionals. Donors aren't ATMs but are first and foremost friends, teammates, and partners. Brad's own development as a friend and partner-raiser is an exciting journey that will lift your hopes and vision sky high. Brad and his FOCUS Group have been friends and true partners with the incredible work of Union Rescue Mission on Skid Row, with life- and career-changing training provided to donor officers as well as completion of a $55 million capital campaign, allowing us to decentralize Skid Row services and regionalize them throughout LA County."

Andrew J. Bales, president and CEO of Union Rescue Mission in Los Angeles

"Given the whirlwind of ideas and advice out there about nonprofit fundraising, with *Turning Donors into Partners* Brad Layland has now cleared the air. Centered around a single principle—know your donors and maintain relationships with them—Brad offers some of the most powerful, practical, and concisely written advice I have ever found on partnership development. In his own life work and now through successfully coaching others, including the organization I lead, Brad seems to live these principles almost effortlessly. He knows what he is talking about."

Doug Gehman, president of Globe International and author of *Before You Quit*

"I engaged The FOCUS Group for a highly successful capital campaign several years ago, and it is great to see how Brad Layland's substantial expertise translates to the written page. His perspective on donors as partners has helped transform our fundraising ethos, strategies, and practices at Fellowship of Christians in Universities and Schools—and our entire community is better for it!"

Dan Walker, executive director of Fellowship of Christians in Universities and Schools

"I have had the great pleasure of learning from Brad Layland and The FOCUS Group as I stepped into development with no experience. Layland's caring heart for those who give resonated with me and allowed me freedom to be authentic with partners, putting their needs above the money while still fully funding the work. Read this book and learn from one of the best, who has lived these experiences and teaches others from proven success."

Beth Greco, CEO and president of Hoving Home

"Overcoming the invisible barriers and perceptions of fundraising is so necessary in the nonprofit world. Brad's book does just this! With timeless principles, great stories, and practical tips, you will come away with great optimism, hope, and confidence. I have known Brad for the past ten years, and he has been instrumental with our organization in raising up more and more partners around our country."

David Thakkar, president of Young Life of Canada

"If you are ready for a fresh take on fundraising, then *Turning Donors into Partners* is the book you have been looking for. Filled with transformational insights and practical ideas, it is sure to become a resource you return to year after year."

Mandy Arioto, president and CEO of MOPS International

"As the fundraising industry continues to change, Brad Layland reminds us that relationships will always be at the center of any meaningful charitable endeavor. His relational wisdom and integrity are precisely what this industry needs to flourish. This book is a must-read for both executive leaders and development professionals!"

Eric Cook, president of the Society for Classical Learning

TURNING
D NORS
INT

Principles for
Fundraising You'll
Actually Enjoy

PARTNERS

Brad Layland

Foreword by
Tom Lin

An imprint of InterVarsity Press
Downers Grove, Illinois

InterVarsity Press
P.O. Box 1400 | Downers Grove, IL 60515-1426
ivpress.com | email@ivpress.com

InterVarsity Press® is the publishing division of InterVarsity Christian Fellowship/USA®. For more information, visit intervarsity.org.

Scripture quotations, unless otherwise noted, are from The Holy Bible, English Standard Version, copyright © 2001 by Crossway Bibles, a division of Good News Publishers. Used by permission. All rights reserved.

While any stories in this book are true, some names and identifying information may have been changed to protect the privacy of individuals.

The publisher cannot verify the accuracy or functionality of website URLs used in this book beyond the date of publication.

Cover design and image composite: Cindy Kiple
Interior design: Daniel van Loon

ISBN 978-1-5140-0578-1 (print) | ISBN 978-1-5140-0579-8 (digital)

Printed in the United States of America ♾

Library of Congress Cataloging-in-Publication Data
A catalog record for this book is available from the Library of Congress.

30 29 28 27 26 25 24 23 | 12 11 10 9 8 7 6 5 4 3 2 1

I would like to dedicate this book to the greatest evidence

of God's love for me—my sweet and amazing wife.

She is my best friend and believes in me

when I don't believe in myself. I can't imagine life

without her, and I love her dearly.

CONTENTS

FOREWORD

TOM LIN

When I was twenty-four years old, two words—*I want*—changed how I viewed fundraising.

At the time, I was a new InterVarsity campus minister coordinating ministry on several Boston-area campuses. One day, a friend I had never before asked for financial support surprised me by approaching me as I was leaving my house. She handed me a check and told me, "I love the work you're doing here. And I want to give $10,000 to support you and invest in this ministry." I was shocked!

Until that moment, I mostly thought fundraising was about begging for money, as if I wasn't deserving, and that donors would give only if they were feeling merciful. But at that moment, those two words, *I want*, flipped my mindset completely.

I realized: *It isn't about a donor's gift. It's about the sacred hope behind it.*

Donors *want* to be generous. They *want* to follow the Lord's will and *want* to invest in ministries and people who change lives. Their gift expresses a holy *I want* that God has placed in their heart—a sacred hope that they, too, can have an impact for his kingdom. As a ministry or nonprofit, we have the high honor of helping donors fulfill those hopes. It's a calling that is so much deeper, richer, and more satisfying than just "raising more money."

I was thrilled when I heard Brad was writing a book to share his Taking Donors Seriously® framework. Brad isn't just a dear friend; he's also one of the most gifted fundraising professionals I've ever met. His leadership, wisdom, and experience have helped countless organizations take huge steps forward in resourcing their missions—including InterVarsity Christian Fellowship/USA, the organization I serve as president and CEO.

When Brad came to help us start our major giving program, we weren't confident we could raise much of anything. We set an $8 million goal for our first campaign and ended up raising $20 million. In our most recent campaign, we set a target of $81 million and exceeded that too! Those results would have been impossible without Brad's expertise. Because of him, the gospel has reached more students, faculty, and campuses than ever, and our donors have seen the impact of their gifts multiply.

Brad gets that fundraising is ministry like no one else I know. He truly loves the sacred hopes that God has placed in the hearts of donors and organizations alike, and he wants to help everyone in the fundraising relationship fulfill them.

If any of that sounds like an *I want* that's beating in your heart, you're holding the right book. And you're ready to join Brad on this journey of appreciating donors, serving each other, and becoming joy-filled partners on mission together.

INTRODUCTION

In the early 1990s, I was attending the University of Florida, working as a repossession man for two companies, and volunteering as a Young Life leader. My area director at Young Life suggested that instead of being a repo man, I should consider being on student staff with Young Life. He said all I needed to do was raise $5,000. Once I did, I could get paid $500 per month—which meant that I could quit my job as a repo man. So I gave it a try. I sent out ten letters to the parents of my friends from home and waited by the mailbox. After two weeks only $100 had come in, and I was convinced I was going to have to spend the rest of my college career repossessing things from people. I went back to my Young Life staff person and told him that clearly God had not called me into ministry. I was convinced that fundraising wasn't for me and I wasn't good at it.

Fundamentally, I had approached fundraising entirely wrong; instead of pursuing people relationally to raise money, I sent them letters in the mail. Why is it that the ministry I was a part of with high school students was all about building relationships, yet I approached fundraising highly transactionally?

How did Jesus accomplish his ministry? He accomplished his ministry in community. He chose twelve people to transform the world. Fundraising, as you learn in this book, is best done in community with other people that God has called you to do fundraising with. You think what you need is money, but what you really need are partners to walk alongside of you, and together you can change the world. I understand that this is a paradigm shift for many who are reading this book; I assure you that it was a paradigm shift for me.

Fundraising done as a transaction is not fun and not easy to pull off. Each transaction relies on the next transaction to be better or more effective when, in fact, if you seek the relationship with your donors, they will become your partners—making fundraising a joy.

The good news is that my Young Life staff person said, "I just heard about a new fundraising training program that Young Life is starting to use. It's called Taking Donors Seriously (TDS). Why don't you come with me to the upcoming training?"

Taking Donors Seriously turned out to be a principle-based fundraising program developed by an organization called The FOCUS Group. They had licensed the program to Young Life and, after a successful beta test in the Pacific Northwest, Young Life had begun rolling out the training to areas across the country. I still have my notes from that original training, from long before a Taking Donors Seriously manual was ever developed.

When I got home from the training, I implemented what I heard and quickly raised the $5,000. Later, when the founder of The FOCUS Group was ready to retire, I was able to purchase The FOCUS Group and the rights to Taking Donors

Seriously and ultimately become the person who is responsible for stewarding these excellent tools. I am confident you will find the same success that I have using TDS.

But the goal of this book is *not* to make your life easier and to help you have more funds so you are simply less stressed— the goal of this book is to help you have the funds you need to fulfill the mission that you are called to!

DOING IT DIFFERENTLY

AN INTRODUCTION TO TAKING DONORS SERIOUSLY

Several years ago, I was intrigued by a party game I saw. Three people from the party are sent out of the room. Then the first person is brought back into the room and given an assignment: pretend to be washing an elephant.

While the first person is miming an elephant bath, the second person is brought back in. With no explanation, the second person is assigned to do what they see the first person doing. By the time the third person comes in and is told to do what the second person is doing, everyone in the crowd is dying with laughter. The first person kind of looks like they could be washing an elephant, but the second person, who's just mimicking them, looks totally ridiculous. But even the second person looks relatively normal compared to the third person, who has absolutely no framework for what they are supposed to be doing.

Fundraising is a lot like this party game. Many people who work in fundraising and development are simply mimicking what they see other people doing. They don't understand why they are doing what they are doing—they just know it is supposed to work because other people are doing it.

Fundraising can be a bewildering process, but it doesn't have to be. Taking Donors Seriously is the framework that explains the *how* behind fundraising efforts. Once you understand the framework (in the game it was washing an elephant), it becomes doable to raise the money organizations need in order to thrive.

ESCAPING THE TREADMILL

I have often compared fundraising to running on a treadmill: relentless forward motion but going nowhere. If you look at what most people do, you will see the annual fundraising dinner with an auction, an end-of-year appeal letter, and possibly a golf tournament. Then it's time to start planning for next year's events, which need to be even better than last year's.

Sure, hopping on a treadmill is a great way to go for a five-mile run without leaving the gym. But nonstop forward motion without going anywhere is no way to live. In the long term, approaching life like this leaves us running ragged, barely noticing our progress because we are so exhausted.

Beyond the obvious disadvantages of focusing on events—draining your staff, exhausting your volunteers, and stressing out the donors themselves—there are some significant problems with this way of fundraising. It's easy to slip into these patterns:

- Having an unrealistic plan to raise the annual budget
- Lacking a fundraising team with clearly defined roles and responsibilities

- Focusing on events instead of relationships
- Lacking strategy to guide how to approach donors, so every donor is approached the same way, regardless of his or her ability and desire to give
- Underutilizing the most effective way to raise money: meeting with donors face-to-face

A BETTER WAY

What if you could achieve your fundraising goal within the first three months of your fiscal year? What if you could raise more money, faster, and with less effort? And what if you could do this while decreasing the pressure on your donors? And most importantly, what if you had more time to advance your organization's mission?

A strategic, relational framework like Taking Donors Seriously helps you jump off the treadmill and move toward a bigger, more sustainable, and less labor-intensive fundraising program. The Taking Donors Seriously framework enables you to establish a strong foundation, with the following elements in place to sustain your fundraising efforts:

- A well-defined annual fundraising plan
- A tangible case for support, a *case statement*, that enables you to clearly share the vision with major donors
- A prioritized list of donors who are likely to support you, based on their relationship with you or your organization
- A strategic and personalized approach for every prospective donor, allowing you to spend most of your time with the donors who will give the majority of the money

- A volunteer fundraising team with specific roles and responsibilities

Many times people have told me that I make fundraising sound simple. The truth is that fundraising *is* simple, but does require hard work, and the hard work is only effective if done the right way. This book will teach you the right way and give you a set of principles to follow when new situations and questions arise.

PEOPLE ARE THE BIGGEST GIVERS

When you read headlines about big corporate donations or giant foundations giving millions of dollars to major causes, you might think that these large entities are the source of most of the giving in America. The truth is, the vast majority of charitable giving is from individuals like you and me! Each year an organization called Giving USA publishes a report on total charitable giving in the United States. In 2020, Americans gave away more than $471 billion.[1] (Billion! As in a thousand million!)

This total amount has gone up every year, except two, since the data has been tracked, and continued through the pandemic. Let's look at how this breaks down by giving type: During 2020, individual people contributed about 69 percent of charitable giving in the United States; almost three quarters! Foundations gave 19 percent of the money. Bequests or estate gifts made up 9 percent of the money, and corporations gave the rest.

The amazing reality is that individuals give a very large part of charitable gifts in the United States. Over $324 billion was given by individual people to organizations like yours. The smallest contributing group of givers is corporations, with about $16.86 billion. So while it is important to think about corporations or foundations, it is most important to think about individuals; that is why it's so important to focus on relationships. Many individuals give six- or even seven-figure gifts, and they don't just give to the biggest, loudest nonprofits. Rather, they give to the causes that have won their hearts—and it could be you and your organization.

START WITH WHO, NOT WHAT

When I was growing up, we had a Hoover vacuum cleaner. It was big, it was heavy, and it didn't work very well—that's what I remember.

In the early 1990s, in the midst of rapid technological innovation and the rise of the global internet, a teacher from the United Kingdom named Jim Dyson got frustrated with his vacuum cleaner. In the midst of so much innovation, surely there was a way to build a better vacuum.

Dyson was able to invent a new vacuum cleaner that used cyclonic separation—and it was a huge improvement over existing vacuum cleaners. But then he tried to find investors. Imagine going into a bank to raise venture capital to start a vacuum cleaner business while everyone else is trying to join the dot-com revolution! He ultimately couldn't get anyone to invest in his business in the UK and wound up going all the way to Japan to find people interested in his vacuum.

In the end, Jim was successful. My wife and I even have a Dyson vacuum cleaner at our house, and it works great! In 2021, Dyson's company, which has expanded into many other technologies, did $6.72 billion (USD) in sales while employing a global workforce of over twelve thousand employees.

It can be hard to trade in our usual way of looking at things, but as Dyson's story attests, sometimes we simply need to do something familiar in a different way.

What does it mean to "build a better vacuum" in fundraising? We must start by asking better questions and rethinking our mindset. I have often said that fundraising is not that complicated; the formula for successful fundraising is simple. At the core, fundraising is about building relationships with individuals and inviting them to be a partner in the mission and vision of your organization. But somehow, the old, familiar ways of thinking about fundraising can sneak up on us. Recently I met with a board of a small nonprofit that does incredible work in our community. When the topic of fundraising came up, they did the equivalent of buying an old vacuum. They started off with that all-too-familiar question: "What are we going to do this year to raise money?"

At face value, this seems like a good question; but in reality, this is the wrong question for a board to be asking. Having a strategy of "what to do" does not take the relational core of fundraising into account. The right question for a board or executive director of an organization to ask is, Who are the people we need to engage with to raise the money we need in order to accomplish the mission and vision of our organization?

This question requires us to know not only the cost of doing our work but also the people who would like to partner with us to accomplish this mission. Our fundraising planning should start with the *who*, not the *what*.

SIX KEY PRINCIPLES OF FUNDRAISING

Our goal is to take donors seriously, but how exactly do we do that? How do we shift from transactional fundraising to relational fundraising? How do we create long-term relationships where people feel like a part of the organization—because they are?

The principles in this chapter enable us to care for people again; we no longer need to be focused on tactics that get them to open their wallets. We may still have a fundraising event like a gala, but when planning out the year, we don't start with the event. Because our goal is to treat people as human beings rather than ATMs, we will instead start by inviting them to share and invest in our organizations.

People have said that the six principles are great—but they sound like they are based on a sales technique to close more sales and sell more widgets. This couldn't be further from the truth. The six principles are biblically based, and there are dozens of examples or references in the Bible that support this framework for fundraising. The principles may underwhelm with their simplicity, but don't be fooled: each principle is incredibly important to the long-term health of an organization's fundraising.

There are six principles and they all work together. I want you to memorize these—don't leave any of them out. You need to be thinking about them continually, returning to them over and over as you fundraise. As you absorb and practice these six key principles, you will gain a framework for making all decisions related to funding your organization, which will translate into making a bigger difference in your community.

PRINCIPLE 1: PEOPLE GIVE TO PEOPLE THEY KNOW AND TRUST

Fundraising is all about relationships. Without relationships, fundraising simply doesn't work. Over the last twenty-five years of doing fundraising training, hundreds of people have suggested to me that their fundraising problems would be solved if they could just ask Oprah for a gift. But if you send Oprah a letter, asking for money for your organization, what's going to happen? Well, unless you are friends with Oprah, she's not going to say yes to your request. Oprah doesn't have a relationship with you, so she has no reason to give, even if she may agree with your mission.

Having said this, once when I used this example in a large group of people at a fundraising training, a person in the back of the room raised her hand. She said, "I used to be Oprah's executive producer." I laughed and told her that yes, in that case, it was likely that Oprah would actually give her a gift!

If I go to a friend or neighbor and share with them the vision of something I'm involved with, they're much more likely to say yes. There is a little boy in my neighborhood who once or twice a year comes to my house to sell me something. Cookies, magazines, raffle tickets—it could be anything—but whatever he is selling I'm buying, because he is my neighbor. However, if a total stranger comes to my door—even if he is selling something that I want—I am very likely to say no. The relationship is what leads to trust, and trust enables me to say yes.

While I was at Fuller Theological Seminary getting my master of arts in theology, I took a series of systematic theology classes. I was expecting to be a bit bored in Systematic Theology 101, but instead I was blown away by the fundraising insight I got from the course. In that class the professor highlighted the fact that God, at his very center, is a relational God. God only exists as Father, Son, and Holy Spirit, in relationship with one another. When we are in relationships with our spouse, friends, and associates, we are modeling the core of who God is. Therefore, when we create a relationally based fundraising plan, we are modeling our fundraising after the very essence of God!

About twenty years ago, I went to the post office and opened the PO box to discover a check in the mail for the small nonprofit I was leading. The check was for $1,000 from a foundation I had never heard of. Since my organization's budget added up to a grand total of $40,000 a year, this was a big deal; this check would make a huge difference. Hurrying back to my office, I immediately looked up the foundation. I called to see if I could meet with them and do two things—first, thank them; and second, ask them why they were choosing to give to our organization.

The foundation put me in touch with a man named Bill Thurman. Bill had been put in charge of giving away money to organizations that were serving young people, and he had simply stumbled across our organization. I called up Bill and asked if we could get together. He agreed, and a few weeks later I met Bill for lunch at a local country club that he had enthusiastically suggested. Over lunch, we talked about two main subjects—our work and clam chowder. It soon became obvious that Bill was extremely fond of clam chowder, and especially the clam chowder at this country club. As we ate, I shared enthusiastically about our organization that served young people, and he shared about his life and the clam chowder.

This was just the first of many clam chowder lunches. Now, the truth is, I don't actually like clam chowder, but my friend Bill liked it so much that I ate clam chowder with him. Over the next several years, I continued to meet Bill at the country club, and he continued to give and raise funds for our organization. Our clam chowder lunches became a bit of a tradition. And over the next several years, Bill's giving went from $1,000 a year to over $50,000 a year.

People give to people they know and trust. Through dozens of bowls of clam chowder, Bill and I got to be friends. Genuine trust was formed, and an amazing partnership was built.

PRINCIPLE 2: PEOPLE GIVE BECAUSE THEY ARE ASKED AND SHOWN HOW

This principle seems obvious on the surface: people give because they are asked and shown how. But the number one reason people give is because they are asked. If you don't ask, normally you don't get anything.

Several years ago, I made a gift to Habitat for Humanity. I didn't know much about the organization, other than the fact that a former president of the United States was very involved with their work. Still, I made a gift. And then the next year I made a second gift because they called me and said, "Will you make another gift?"

Unfortunately, it took me ten years to make my third gift. Why? Because no one asked me during that time. Ten years after my second gift, a person from that organization enrolled in a Taking Donors Seriously training course and saw a video where I gave this example. I mentioned the organization and how I had not given them any more money. After this, someone from the organization asked me again and I gave my third gift.

The second part of this principle is also critical: people give because they are shown how. *Shown how* means that donors understand how they fit into the overall fundraising efforts of the organization before they make a gift. It's not enough to make someone aware of a need. Donors need to know that there is a plan to raise the whole budget and how their gift will fit into that larger plan—that is fundamentally what it means to show them how. The donor needs to understand how their gift will make a difference in the work of your organization.

As I mentioned, I gave my third gift to Habitat for Humanity when I was asked by a person whose mom took the Taking Donors Seriously course. The amazing thing is, the person who asked me was fourteen years old. Josh raised over $100,000 using the approach described in this book. The following is his story:

I was nine years old, and I heard about a boy named Ryan; he founded the Ryan's Well Foundation, which was trying to raise money to build wells in Africa. He saw people without water, and he wanted to do something about it—that inspired me to do something in the world. The answer came two years later when I was with my dad in the Habitat for Humanity Durham ReStore.

I was in there and I saw a sign for the Habitat for Humanity Pennies for Homes Campaign. They were trying to raise $100,000 to build a house for low-income families—in pennies. So that is 10 million pennies! And instantly I heard God say, "You got to do that!"

I worked at it for a couple years, but it was not going as smoothly as I had planned. I kind of hit a bit of a plateau— I was at $22,000. My original goal was that I would finish in three years. So if it took two years to raise $22,000, how could I raise $78,000 in one year?

My mom and dad were doing a fundraising training with Young Life and they saw this Taking Donors Seriously video. It was Brad talking about an organization that builds houses all around the world that he used to donate to until they stopped asking. And so, he stopped donating. He also said if anyone who was watching the video that is a part of that organization asked him for a donation, he would do so. My mom thought this was a great opportunity. She got Brad's email through Young Life's president, Dave Thakker. Brad received the email and said he would give me a twelve-week TDS course and also a $500 donation in the end. So we ran with that.

I started my TDS training. It was amazing. I learned so much about fundraising that I had no idea existed. But it all makes sense. I went through it and learned that I had to meet with people to get donations. But I was fourteen years old and there are big scary adults in the world. Would adults be willing to meet with me? What am I supposed to be like, "Hey, let's go get some coffee and talk about giving me some money?" I even felt greedy because some of them had already given me pennies. Would they give me more money?

Through the course I gained confidence, and another thing I also learned about was making a team of people, very dedicated people, who were involved in the community, to make things happen that I could not make happen. And so, taking those two things together, I met with people. I raised the money that way. People responded to that, which was amazing. And it actually worked. It all worked amazing, and I raised the extra $78,000 I needed to raise to build a house.[1]

Josh was successful because he invited people to give and showed them how to give!

In the Old Testament there is a great example of this second principle. Nehemiah is trying to rebuild the wall in Jerusalem and goes to the king to get supplies.

The king said to me, "What is it you want?" Then I prayed to the God of heaven, and I answered the king, "If it pleases the king and if your servant has found favor in his sight, let him send me to the city in Judah where my ancestors are buried so that I can rebuild it." Then the king, with the queen sitting beside him, asked me, "How long will your journey take, and when will you get back?" It pleased the king to send me; so I set a time. I also said to him, "If it pleases the king, may I have letters to the governors of Trans-Euphrates, so that they will provide me safe-conduct until I arrive in Judah? And may I have a letter to Asaph, keeper of the royal park, so he will give me timber to make beams for the gates of the citadel by the temple and for the city wall and for the residence I will occupy?" And because the gracious hand of my God was on me, the king granted my requests. (Nehemiah 2:4-8 NIV)

Nehemiah knows exactly what he wants, and he comes to the king prepared. Nehemiah clearly asks and shows how. He says, "Will you support me? And I need letters for specific things."

There is one other thing I love here. It says in verse six that the queen was sitting beside him. I love that Nehemiah knew he should ask the king with the queen there. We should ask the couple when they are together. We shouldn't just ask the man or the woman, but we should ask them both.

PRINCIPLE 3: PEOPLE GIVE WHEN THEY'RE INVOLVED AND HAVE A SENSE OF OWNERSHIP

Take a moment to think about the causes and organizations you consistently give to. Is it the school your kids attend? The organization you were involved in during college? The shelter where you adopted your pets? When we examine our own giving, we usually find a connection. Yet sometimes we forget to cultivate this connection and involve our donors.

A few years ago, I got the chance to meet with a major donor on behalf of one of my clients. Earlier that year, the donor had given generously to this organization at their annual fundraising gala. The gift was much larger than a typical gift, which is the reason that I met with him in the first place. But as I sat and talked with him and his wife, I realized that while the gift was big for this organization, it was much smaller than this donor's usual mega gifts to other organizations. He told me that he had helped pay for a dorm at his children's school with a very large gift. I asked him why he had given a smaller gift to our client while giving so much to the school. His answer? He explained that his only interaction with our client was getting invited to a fundraising gala each year.

Once my client and I realized this, my client began to invest a significant amount of time in this donor. Over the next two years, my client made trips to this donor's house, spent time with his family, and got to know his hobbies. Most importantly, the donor and his family members were invited to come and see the work our client was doing. Through these interactions, this donor's giving increased until he is now my client's largest donor. This situation reminds me of my passion for running—specifically running marathons.

I ran my first marathon at twenty-nine years old. I thought it would be amazing to simply complete a marathon. My first marathon clocked in at five hours, forty-five minutes. I was so excited about finishing that I bought the plaque with my picture and the time on the clock. Since I was new to running, I had no perspective on whether a 5:45 marathon was fast or slow. I quickly learned that my pace was slow when I showed my plaque to my running friends. Anyone that finishes a marathon in any amount of time should be incredibly proud, but I learned that the world record for a marathon is just over two hours. After that I set a goal to run a marathon in under four hours.

In 2020, I hit my goal. It took me sixteen years and twenty-four marathons. That's over 628 miles of racing, and weeks and weeks of training runs, but I finally did it. Along that journey I ran a marathon in Dubai with a first-time marathoner from Ethiopia who was only eighteen years old. On his very first marathon he won the race, finishing in 2:04:32. It was incredible that Tsegaye Mekonnen won the 2014 Dubai Marathon with such a fast time—but running a marathon for the first time and winning almost never happens.[2]

Maybe you have heard about some person raising a huge sum of money very easily, and their success might make you feel like a failure. These are exceptions—when people raise a ton of money easily or run really fast their first time—these are outliers to the norm. Running fast marathons is a lot like raising money and working with major donors. Training to run a marathon fast, and fundraising, takes time. If you truly care about people and relationships, you have to invest time and put in a lot of miles to get the right results, just like training for a marathon. I challenge you to think of fundraising as a long journey, not a quick sprint, because people give when they are involved and have a sense of ownership.

In the Bible, there are dozens of times God involves people in the work he is accomplishing on earth. For example, in John 21:6, Jesus begins to reveal to the disciples who he really is—not by telling them who he is, but by showing them who he is. He tells them where the fish are: "Cast the net on the right side of the boat, and you will find some." So they cast it and they are not able to haul it in because of the quantity of fish.

Also in the Old Testament, when God asks Noah to build an ark to save his people, he invites Noah into his work. Did God really need Noah's boat? Couldn't God just snap his fingers and accomplish the same thing?

Once the disciples and Noah were a part of what God was doing, their perspective on what was happening was different. The same is true when we involve our donors in our work.

PRINCIPLE 4: GIVING IS A WAY OF LIFE

Some people simply have the gift of giving. My work constantly brings me into contact with people who are givers. It is a joy to meet people who possess the gift of giving. I have learned to realize that the gift of giving is a spiritual gift. Paul says in Romans 12,

> For just as each of us has one body with many members, and these members do not all have the same function, so in Christ we, though many, form one body, and each member belongs to all the others. We have different gifts, according to the grace given to each of us. If your gift is prophesying, then prophesy in accordance with you faith; if it is serving, then serve; if it is teaching, then teach; if it is to encourage, then give encouragement; if it is giving, then give generously; if it is to lead, do it diligently; if it is to show mercy, do it cheerfully. (Romans 12:4-8 NIV)

As Paul says in verse 8—giving is a spiritual gift. I believe that all of us are called to give, but some people have an extraordinary ability and desire to be a giver!

I got the chance to meet a donor who has the gift of giving. I met him at one of his houses. He is a donor to many of the clients we serve at The FOCUS Group. During our meeting, he shared with me that he and his wife had come to a pivotal moment a few years ago. They realized that they had all they needed, enough both for themselves and for their children. In light of this realization, the couple made a decision: they would give everything else away. With the decision made, the man got to work giving away the rest of their money. He got to the point where he supports over one hundred organizations—ten of which he supports at over $100,000 a year. He then went on to say, though, that this goal of giving everything else away had been one of the biggest failures of his life.

I asked him why he had failed. Had he begun to hold back? "No," he said. "I am a failure because God seems to be blessing me with more. Despite my near reckless giving, my net worth has tripled."

I do not believe in a "prosperity gospel" in which by giving we get more, but I do believe that when we allow God to use us as conduits of his resources, we are blessed (in more ways than just more money). My friend was having difficulty giving it all away! Giving is simply a way of life for some people, and God seems to bless people.

Another person who had the gift of giving was Charles Feeney. Charles made his money by setting up duty-free shops in airports around the world. He came up with the idea after being in World War II and seeing the unique opportunity. Charles made an extraordinary amount of money, and when he was fifty-one years old he sold his company for approximately $500 million. He then invested the money in multiple ways and leveraged his large fortune into a huge fortune of $8.5 billion dollars. He formed a foundation and began giving his money away.

Charles was a simple man, and until he was seventy-five years old he had only traveled in coach on airplanes. He always tried to give in secrecy because he wanted to allow others to get the naming rights so as to leverage his gifts. He had two goals—to give away half of his fortune by 2016, and to give away all of his money by 2020. He accomplished his goal.[3] Currently Charles is ninety years old and is living in a rented San Francisco apartment and has a net worth of approximately $2 million.[4]

When you find a person who has the gift of giving—like my friend or Charles Feeney—invest your time to get to know them and get them involved with your organization. Over time they will blow you away with their generosity. They're going to give you money, they're going to give you their time, they might let you stay in their vacation home, and they might even do shocking things like pay for your kids to go to college (this really happened to the executive director of one of my clients).

Do I believe that God rewards givers by giving them more when they give recklessly? No! But I do believe that generosity frees givers to make decisions that allow them to steward more resources than those people who are not givers.

Holding on to all that we have traps us; it certainly does not allow us to experience the joy of being generous. Givers find incredible joy through giving. Is it possible that the joy that givers find from giving translates into them being happier, which makes them more effective professionally, allowing them to make more money? It's worth thinking about. As for me, I'd love to get stuck in that cycle. Wouldn't you?

PRINCIPLE 5: A NO IS NEVER FOREVER

People often have good reasons why they don't give. Don't take it personally. When you receive a no from a prospective or previous donor to your organization, trust that there is a context for that no. Even if you're already taking good care of your relationships with prospective donors, you may not be privy to the most recent events in their lives. That life event you aren't aware of could be preventing them from giving right now.

My years of experience have shown me that if I listen and follow up, I will eventually receive a gift. You must remember that a *no* does not mean "never." If a donor takes a meeting with you and then says they can't give right now, be patient. There is a reason they took the meeting with you, and a reason they can't give right now. It is all going to be okay in the end; you just need to understand the no, and realize that no has a context.

A few years ago, a friend of mine needed to raise several million dollars to build a new camp for Young Life. He was friends with a woman who he knew had a passion for Young Life and had given multiple times to help build other Young Life camps. My friend called her to ask about meeting with her to tell her about the new camp. Much to my friend's surprise, she responded by saying that she had given all her money away to a large seminary. Although my friend was discouraged, he knew that meeting with her and sharing about the new camp would still be fun. He decided to go and meet with her anyway, especially since she had been such a faithful donor in the past. He went to her house, and over tea and cookies he told her all about the vision for the new camp. As he left that day, the woman commented, "I know I said that I have given all my money to the seminary, but I haven't given all of my money— it's just that I can't give a gift until next calendar year."

In this case, the person's response had a context. She was not trying to communicate that she would never give again to the organization, just that she was already fully committed for the current calendar year. Because my friend chose to understand the no, he learned that there was a context for that response—and a context for the yes that he received the following calendar year. Every no has a context and we must spend the time to understand that context!

I am so glad that God is a loving, patient God who lives out this principle perfectly. God created our world perfect, but we chose to turn our back on God and say no to him. Our no earned us eternal separation (Romans 3:23), but our no is not forever, due to Jesus' work on the cross. Romans 6:23 says that "the wages of sin is death, but the free gift of God is eternal life in Christ Jesus our Lord." When we said no to God, he found a way to bring us back into a relationship with him. So despite the fact that sometimes a donor says no, stay engaged, like God does with us, and commit to better understand the context of your donor's no.

PRINCIPLE 6: PROPER PLANNING MAXIMIZES RESULTS AND MINIMIZES COSTS

Planning is often an area of struggle for nonprofits. We get busy and we forget to plan. We get so busy doing the next thing that we forget to do the best thing; we must slow down and think about the most important thing to do. Should we focus on the donor who could give us $50 a month, or the donor who could give us $5,000? Our natural tendency is to get so caught up in the busyness of the day that we don't plan out or prioritize the most important things. We have to ask: Who is actually giving the majority of the money to our organization?

If we look carefully at the numbers, we will see that a small number of donors do most of the total giving, and a larger number of donors do a small portion of the giving. In Taking

Donors Seriously, we emphasize taking all our donors seriously, treating each of them with care. However, that does not mean treating all donors the same. We should absolutely care for people that can give only $10; yes—we need to thank them! But if there is a donor that can give $10,000 and that gift means caring for a hundred homeless people, opening a new animal shelter, or repairing homes for low-income seniors, wouldn't we want to spend more of our time and resources connecting with the $10,000 donor? We need to consider which few donors can help our organization do its best, and plan to invest in them and follow up with them consistently.

God sent his Son in response to our no, but it wasn't without an entire Bible-full of planning. I heard a sermon once where the pastor opened up the Bible and read from Genesis 1: "In the beginning God created the heavens and the earth." He then turned the page and read about Adam and Eve disobeying God and eating the forbidden fruit. He then held up the rest of the Bible and said, "This is the story of what God did to give you the opportunity to be in relationship with him." Two pages of the Bible is the original plan; the rest of the Bible is the story of God's careful planning on sending his Son to earth for us to be given the chance to know him. My challenge is for us to model our fundraising plans on that level of precision. The work we are doing is important and strategic, therefore our fundraising should be as well.

Several years ago, I walked into the office of a nonprofit, and on the desk of the executive director (ED) was a huge stack of gift receipts. During the meeting, the ED shared with me that he was committed to personally thanking every donor who gave any amount to their organization. I asked him how he did that and he said that he signed every gift receipt personally and wrote notes on all of them. The follow-up question I asked him was, "What else do you do to care for your donors?" He replied that he didn't have time to do anything else beyond signing these receipts and running the ministry.

While his intent was amazing, his execution of the principle was wrong and not the best use of his time. While it is extremely important to thank donors, signing every gift receipt is not the best use of an executive director's time. A more effective and efficient thing for that executive director to do would be to spend time meeting with his largest donors in face-to-face meetings and then have the gift receipts processed and mailed out. While a hand-signed note is great, a personal face-to-face thank you is better! Done well, planning maximizes results and minimizes costs.

For a downloadable PDF summary of the six principles and other resources go to TheFocusGroup.com/partners.

THE TAKING DONORS
SERIOUSLY FRAMEWORK

Years ago when I was in college, my best friend and I set out on a six-thousand-mile trip across the country. We traveled from Florida to the West Coast, and back home through Chicago. The year was 1993 and we did it all without a global positioning system (GPS). How did we do it? Not by following the sun! We used a map and followed road signs, but there was no Siri to direct us. The trip was amazing, but since we did not have a GPS we made lots of wrong turns that often found us going in the wrong direction. Technically we could have followed the sun, but that would have been even worse than following the maps. Fundraising is a lot like that trip across the country: there is a best way—GPS—and there is a less efficient way—following the sun.

Technically, on a road trip we can just jump in the car and head west, but why would we when we can say, "Hey Siri, please take me to Los Angeles"? In the same way, fundraising is most efficient when we have a basic framework to build on. There are five fundamentals that are the centerpiece of all fundraising. By adopting these building blocks, our fundraising journey will be much easier and more efficient than simply doing what others are doing (following the sun on a road trip).

The following is a brief introduction to the Taking Donors Seriously framework. Each of these items will be described in greater detail in the following chapters.

CASE

The *case* for support is a written document that answers these questions: Why does your organization exist? What problem are you trying to solve? How much do you need to raise to accomplish these goals? This document is the first component of the framework.

The case tells your story in a compelling way with text, photos, and graphics. You will use the case to clearly articulate your mission, programs, financial needs, and overall plan. Often, the exercise of gathering the data and preparing the case statement enables organizations to be more focused and unified. This is a great side effect!

Your leaders will use the case statement as a presentation tool when meeting with donors. The case statement also helps your organization to have a unified voice, reiterating a consistent message in every newsletter, marketing communication, event, and donor visit.

LEADERSHIP

The case is a printed piece of material, but it won't raise any money sitting on a shelf! It needs legs. Your *leadership* is the second component of the framework. Your staff and volunteers will take the case out into the world, sharing with other people the impact of what you are doing.

Remember the principle, people give to those they know and trust. There is a direct relationship between the giving power of your donors and the strength of your leadership. Whether your leaders are the executive director, staff, volunteers, or on the board of directors, activating them means knowing them well enough to identify their gifts. Recognizing each person's gifts allows you to ask people to serve in roles where they will be most effective. As a result, your organization will have leadership for every type of venture, from one-on-one visits to large-scale events.

PROSPECTS

Once you have identified and activated your leadership, they will connect to your prospective givers. Your *prospects* are the third component of the Taking Donors Seriously framework.

This may sound simple, but to take donors seriously, you have to know who they are! Part of this process is to make a list of all your prospects. Then you will organize the list using specific characteristics to produce a priority prospect list (PPL). Is this person a new donor? Are they a longtime returning donor? Do they love what you do already? The PPL will tell you all of this information at a glance.

Prioritizing prospects has to do with understanding who they are in terms of interest, financial ability, and inclination to give. Assembling information on these three criteria enables you to prioritize your prospects, whether individuals, foundations, or businesses.

STRATEGY

To use your time prudently, you will need to be strategic. Which fundraising approaches are the best use of your time? *Strategy*, the fourth component of this framework, boils down to two concepts: efficiency and effectiveness.

Are you just trying to get it all done as quickly as possible? That probably won't be very effective, but it is efficient. Or you could meet with every donor personally, which would be very effective but not at all efficient. How do you decide which donors to prioritize for personal meetings? Do you really have time to meet one-on-one with every prospect? We will discuss the 80/20 rule in greater detail in chapter seven, allowing it to shed light on how best to use your limited time. The good news is, streamlining your strategy will also streamline your schedule!

PLAN

Once you have a strategy about how to approach each person on your prospect list, you will lay it out on an actual calendar. This is the fifth component of the Taking Donors Seriously framework: the financial master *plan*. This plan will spell out all your efforts toward donor care—individual meetings as well as events and group methods, such as small groups, banquets, and communication.

Your plan allows you to work strategically during the entire calendar year, one month at a time. In chapter nine, the fundraising plan, you'll learn which donors to prioritize earlier in the year, and how to expand your focus to the entire donor base later in the year.

When all the elements of the Taking Donors Seriously framework work together, they make fundraising both effective and efficient.

These components must be arranged properly. Imagine trying to bake a cake by putting just the eggs in the oven for 45 minutes, then stirring in the other ingredients: the flour, sugar, butter, water, and so on. Even though you have the right ingredients, no cake will result from that process! Fundraising is similar: you not only need the right ingredients, but you must also arrange them properly to work together. The next chapters will equip you to do just that.

For a downloadable PDF summary of the TDS framework and other resources, go to TheFocusGroup.com/partners.

PRACTICE 1
THE CASE STATEMENT

Your organization has a dream, a vision of what it's trying to do. You've identified a problem in the world, and you've come up with a way to address it. You've even figured out how you're going to do it and how much it's going to cost. You're going out into the world and saying, "Fund our mission! Fund our organization! Fund me!" The case statement is the tool that makes it happen.

The case statement is the first component of the Taking Donors Seriously framework. It can be a challenge to develop a case, but once you really pour yourself into it and develop one, it can be incredibly motivating to you and your donors. Keep in mind this is not a brochure, although it may look like one. The case functions as a dynamic presentation tool as you talk about your organization and ask for support. It's a chance to communicate to individual donors the way you think about your mission and your organization. When you approach the case this way, you gain a serious fundraising tool that will help you navigate conversations about your funding needs.

The case is intended specifically for individual donors, the case is not something sent in a mailing or passed out to a large group. The case is designed to be shared in one-on-one meetings, whether with an individual, a couple, or the board of a foundation. However, you may use elements of the case as material for future mailings, a program for a banquet, a brochure, or other documents designed for group settings.

The case statement functions both horizontally and vertically. It is horizontal in that it can give a sweeping thirty-thousand-foot view when necessary, but at the same time it is vertical in that the case should allow you to drill down into the details when appropriate. If you are meeting with someone who is not very familiar with your organization, rather than a current donor, you should use the case statement horizontally. When you are meeting with someone who already knows quite a bit about your organization and has questions about your programs, you should use the case vertically. Give this person more information and go into more detail. Ideally, you are anticipating their questions before the meeting, and planning what to cover in your case presentation that addresses their concerns. It's impressive when you know a donor well enough to anticipate what they might be interested in talking about. Be intentional about knowing who you are trying to engage and whether a horizontal or vertical approach would be more appropriate.

The case statement is as important for the person presenting the vision as for the person receiving the presentation. Preparing the case will organize your thinking and your vision far faster and more comprehensively than any other method I know. If you have clarity about your role and mission in a given community, you will be able to make a logical and compelling argument for your prospective donor's participation.

Some years ago I had prepared a case statement and was using it with a major donor. This donor had a long-held basic understanding of our organization but from an arm's length away. As I met with her and presented the case statement, she came alive, as if for the first time she fully understood what we were trying to do in our community. The meeting ended with her volunteering to serve on our board. She has now been serving on the board for the last twenty-five years. Through the presentation of the case she finally understood the big picture, and she has given thousands of dollars and thousands of hours of her time.

There are ten distinct sections of a case statement. Each section connects with the others in a natural flow of thought. Creativity is important in creating the case, but use extreme caution before rearranging or eliminating any of these sections. The format we recommend is time-tested, proving over and over to be an excellent presentation tool. As you create the actual document, start by giving each section its own separate page. Here are the ten elements of a case:

1. Theme
2. Need
3. Mission
4. Lifetime value
5. Program

6. Accomplishments
7. Vision
8. Budget
9. Gift plan
10. Profile of leadership

CASE STATEMENT SECTION 1: THEME

As you open the case statement, the first page (the title page, or splash page) features the theme. The theme is the central message your organization is trying to communicate. It distills into a compelling, one-line phrase what your organization is doing in the community. It usually contains an action verb such as *changing, bringing,* or *restoring.* Here are some examples:

Increasing volunteering (Volunteer Match)

Feeding the hungry (Food Pantries for the Capital District)

Restoring hope (Union Rescue Mission)

The theme provides a cornerstone for the case, and this one-line phrase is woven throughout the case, both in words and pictures. However, it may take some time to create a clear and concise theme. Here are some general guidelines to help you develop your theme:

- This one-line phrase ideally starts with a verb or gerund and is no more than a few words.

- The theme highlights your organization's niche and its real-life impact.

- The theme takes your audience into account.

Your target audience will become clear when you build your Prospect List, but you probably already know a little bit about them. If your target audience is over the age of sixty but your theme uses language that sounds like a twenty-something wrote it, you will want to adjust it. The theme page also introduces the look and feel of your case, using photos or graphics.

Again, your visuals should engage the audience you are trying to reach.

If your organization provides medical relief in a developing country, then include pictures of the people you are trying to serve. The images shouldn't be so overwhelming or disturbing, however, that people will turn the cover over on their dining room table when you are not around. Instead, the front cover and the theme page should feature pictures that gently, but not manipulatively, reach out and grab the hearts of the people you want to connect with. If you are wondering how to do this, ask a few donors you know well to give feedback about the images you have chosen to represent the work. Ultimately, you are designing this document with your audience in mind.

Knowing your audience will change how you market to them. Perhaps you know someone who is an advertising genius or who is really good at communicating a message; ask that person to help you develop your theme, because in reality there really is a "right" theme that will fit both your mission and your audience. The theme matters deeply because it sets the tone for the whole case statement and will be echoed in each section.

Be open-minded as you go through this process. What do people who don't know you very well say about your organization? Consider not only the organization as you know it but also what an outsider thinks. If your organization flies medical supplies into remote areas of the jungle, how would a stranger describe that? This is an excellent prompt for you to use as you develop your theme.

Let's look at some specific examples. One of our clients chose the theme "Real Grace." This client was a school that wanted to communicate that they offer grace for students who wouldn't otherwise have a loving home. Throughout their case, on each page, every section and heading tied into that theme with words and pictures, showing how the school cared for their students in profound ways, offering life-giving grace to each one of them. Stories and anecdotes from students illustrated that real people were being deeply affected by the work of the school.

A second example comes from the classical school that I helped start in St. Augustine—Veritas Classical School. Their case theme is "Cultivating Hearts, Souls and Minds." If you flip through their case statement, you'll see how Veritas is intentionally educating children in St. Augustine; Veritas is training students to recognize what is true, good, and beautiful, and to understand God's love for them. The theme shows that Veritas is approaching education very differently than what the public school system is doing.

Here is another example: "Creating Hope." This theme was chosen by a team that wanted to reach people with the love of Christ using karaoke in the world's largest unreached country.

Figures 4.1, 4.2, and 4.3 are examples of the cover page of the case statements mentioned above.

CASE STATEMENT SECTION 2: NEED

I know what you're thinking: *Need! How much money do I need? We need lots of it!* But that's not what I mean by pinpointing need.

What is the problem in the world that your organization is addressing? Is it lack of medicine, food, shelter for the homeless,

Figure 4.1. Real grace

or companionship to lonely elderly people? What is broken in the world that you are trying to fix? The needs in your community can often be represented by real numbers: "There are x number of homeless people in our town"; "In our city, three thousand children don't have a hot meal each day." These are the needs your organization gets to address.

Figure 4.2. Cultivating hearts, souls and minds

Often we go to our donors and say, "I need your help with my budget." That's actually not right. The more appropriate statement is, "I need your help in feeding these three thousand hungry kids and letting them know someone cares about them" or "I need your help in providing medicine to these people who have a life-threatening disease." This is a subtle shift but very important.

Figure 4.3. Creating hope

It is important to do your homework to be able to state statistics accurately. You should be able to cite your sources. For instance, "According to *US News and World Report*, there are x many . . ." Don't overstate the problem. It must be based on facts that you have researched.

A field test can help you understand how best to communicate the need. As you explain your need to donors and they begin to respond, you'll learn which statistics are the most compelling. Take notes on what people say. When do they stop and ask, "What? There really are two thousand people who are homeless in my town?" Notice when they are floored by the reality of the numbers: "Is it true that there are six hundred kids in our town whose only meal each day is their lunch at school?"

Recently a client of ours talked with prospective donors about how a significant number of Christian children who grow up in the church walk away from their faith during college. One donor after another read the statistic and asked, "Is that true? Is it true that such a high percentage of children raised in a Christian home walk away from their faith?" Each donor who saw the statistic was stunned. When the organization initially presented the need to their donors, this statistic was listed seventh in a list. After observing donor reactions, the organization realized that this statistic needed to come first, because it was the one that grabbed people's hearts. It was also a statistic that the organization was doing something to change.

Put the most compelling statistics first. You want the ones that hit home to be the first ones donors read. As you state your need, remember these guidelines:

- Don't overstate or overwhelm donors with the need. This is dishonest and may actually discourage donors.

- Do your homework. Use numbers where possible, preferably quoting statistics local to your operations, and be able to cite your sources.

- A field study can test drive the statistics to find out which numbers are the most compelling.

- Place the most compelling statistics first.

- Consider showing the need graphically; a chart or diagram may be easier to understand.

CASE STATEMENT SECTION 3: MISSION

The mission statement is your organization's answer to the need. Your organization should already have a mission statement, so including it in your case is easy. If you have one, you know what I mean—you likely spent a long time in a board room arguing about exactly what that mission statement should contain! Don't re-create the wheel here.

Sometimes organizations have mission statements that are too long and hard to remember. The most compelling ones are about a sentence long and succinctly explain what the organization is trying to accomplish. Here are some favorites:

To rescue millions, protect half a billion, and make justice unstoppable.

To see all affected by crime reconciled to God, their families, and their communities.

Improve lives by mobilizing the caring power of communities around the world to advance the common good.

You might be able to identify these organizations just by reading their mission statements: International Justice Mission,

Prison Fellowship, and United Way. Each statement sums up the purpose of the organization. Ultimately, the appeal for funds will be based on the mission.

If you don't have a mission statement yet, take some time to create one. It should answer the question, Why does your organization exist? Here are a few more examples for inspiration. Some of these express a mission in just a few words!

TED: Ideas Worth Spreading

The Humane Society: Celebrating Animals, Confronting Cruelty

The Smithsonian National Museum of Natural History: Our mission is to promote understanding of the natural world and our place in it.

In response to God's love, grace, and truth: The purpose of InterVarsity Christian Fellowship/USA is to establish and advance at colleges and universities witnessing communities of students and faculty who follow Jesus as Savior and Lord: growing in love for God, God's Word, God's people of every ethnicity and culture, and God's purposes in the world.

Young Life is a mission devoted to introducing adolescents to Jesus Christ and helping them grow in their faith.

CASE STATEMENT SECTION 4: LIFETIME VALUE

The next element of the case statement is what we call the lifetime value of your organization. When people make a big investment in an organization, they don't want to change things just for today—they want to change things for a lifetime, and maybe forever. What is the impact of your organization's work over the course of a lifetime? Answer this with specific examples of people who have been impacted by your organization.

Previously I mentioned an organization whose mission was to reach at-risk teenagers in my town. One of these teenagers is now the city's mayor and another one is the pastor of one of the largest churches. These are great examples of lifetime value. The organization can say, "Teenagers in our organization grow up to be mayors and pastors." To communicate this idea, they would simply tell their stories.

If your organization takes care of orphaned animals, tell the story of the dog who was adopted and now provides companionship for an elderly widow. If your organization provides repairs to low-income homeowners who live in unsafe homes, tell the story of a homemaker who was able to stay—and thrive—in her now-repaired home. If your organization seeks to end AIDS in Africa, then tell the stories of the people in their forties or fifties who are alive due to the work of your organization.

Rather than saying, "In theory, if we do this, then three thousand people will live better lives," focus on telling real stories and showing what has already happened: "If we do this work, it will change this community for the better. There will be people like Smiley Sturgis, who faced an uncertain future as an at-risk teen, but now contributes to his community and serves the city as the pastor of Good News Church."[1] When a person's life is changed through your organization, what do they look like twenty, thirty, or forty years down the road? You are showing that your mission really works.

Recently I witnessed an amazing example of lifetime value. To celebrate fifty years of Young Life in St. Augustine, we invited Bill Heavener, who founded the chapter back in 1969, to our annual banquet.

After Bill spoke, a second speaker, Justine Conley, got up to share about the legacy of Young Life in St. Augustine. During her talk, she asked Bill to come to the front of the room. Then she asked anyone who had been impacted by Bill's ministry to come and stand behind him. Next, she asked anyone who had been impacted by those people's ministries to come and stand behind them. She continued this process until almost every person was standing in the front of the room. It was a beautiful illustration of lifetime value. One life changed can lead to a whole crowd of people whose lives have been transformed!

As you ponder how to illustrate the lifetime value of your organization, think about one life. How is changing this one life going to change your community? You can't see it right now, perhaps, but you know the truth of what I am sharing. You may not know your true impact until years down the road.

I had the chance to see this recently when I visited one of our clients, Pacific Rim Christian University in Honolulu. While visiting this small Christian college, I learned that their former president, Kent M. Keith, was the person who wrote the "Do It Anyway" story that many of us have heard. It was the late sixties when Keith wrote a small booklet that included these lines:

- People are illogical, unreasonable, and self-centered. Love them anyway.

- If you do good, people will accuse you of selfish ulterior motives. Do good anyway.

- If you are successful, you will win false friends and true enemies. Succeed anyway.

- The good you do today will be forgotten tomorrow. Do good anyway.

- Honesty and frankness make you vulnerable. Be honest and frank anyway.

- The biggest men and women with the biggest ideas can be shot down by the smallest men and women with the smallest minds. Think big anyway.

- People favor underdogs but follow only top dogs. Fight for a few underdogs anyway.

- What you spend years building may be destroyed overnight. Build anyway.

- People really need help but may attack you if you do help them. Help people anyway.

- Give the world the best you have, and you will get kicked in the teeth. Give the world the best you have anyway.

These inspiring lines are commonly attributed to Mother Teresa, but she was not the person who wrote them. At some point, someone who knew Mother Teresa pulled these lines from the booklet that Kent Keith wrote. Inspired, Mother Teresa hung them up on her wall, and someone mistakenly attributed them to her. Meanwhile, Kent Keith knew nothing about this until someone sent him his work as a meme—twenty years after he first wrote them! He had no idea that what he had written would inspire Mother Teresa and go viral around the world.[2]

Our work can have long-term effects that are far more powerful than what we dream or imagine. If you happened to write something that inspired Mother Teresa, or your organization happened to rescue J. C. Penney from the streets of New York City (The Bowery Mission did this, long before J. C. Penney started his famous department store), then you should feature those stories.

Most of us don't have stories about Smiley Sturgis, Mother Teresa, or J. C. Penney, but all of us have stories of real people whose lives have been touched, changed, or transformed by the work we are doing. These individuals' stories show the long-term, very real impact that your work will have on the future.

Remember, stories stick because we are wired to remember them. Whenever possible, use the power of stories to illustrate the long-term impact of your organization; include quotes and testimonies from actual people.

Are you starting to see how the case statement's elements are arranged in a logical order? Your theme should flow throughout your case, both in words and in pictures. The theme introduces your message; the need demonstrates why your organization exists; the mission answers the need; and the lifetime value shows that your mission works. And remember, this is a presentation tool, not a brochure.

CASE STATEMENT SECTION 5: PROGRAM

Fifth, the case statement explains the "how" of the mission. This section describes your programs, activities, who you are serving, and how you are serving them. If your mission is to end homelessness in Albuquerque, how are you actually doing that?

Explain the specifics: you build shelters; you provide mentors; or you connect people with the resources they need. Explain how you carry out your mission and describe what makes your organization unique. Your program may involve passing out pamphlets, rescuing animals off the street, or reaching out on the web.

If your organization addresses world hunger, do you send food directly from the United States? Do you buy and distribute the food once you are in those countries? Do you partner with other organizations?

I saw a compelling fundraising piece from an organization seeking monetary donations for Haiti. This organization was focused on providing clean water and communicated candidly about their program. Here's the essence of their explanation:

> Don't give us bottled water. It's actually really expensive to ship bottled water from the United States. Instead, we use your donations in the most cost-conscious way possible, buying bottled water that is in Haiti already. We can buy a hundred bottles of clean water in Haiti for the cost of what one bottle would cost to ship from the US. Our process helps us provide clean water to 99 additional people for the same cost.

This piece was only a page long, including pictures. After reading the page, I immediately understood what they were about. And I promise you, if I want to help people in Haiti, I am never going to give bottles of water to an organization in the United States; I'm going to give them a dollar because that dollar will have a bigger impact. The program section of your case simply describes how you do what you do.

CASE STATEMENT SECTION 6: ACCOMPLISHMENTS

The sixth component of the case statement is accomplishments. It's crucial to show how the organization is doing. This section shows the organization's achievements in a quantitative way. For example, how many graduates did you have? How many people did you find housing for last year? Speaking more generally, how many lives have you changed? You're looking for statistics, especially ones that relate to your organization's impact.

As you communicate the impact of your programs, share data in a way that will capture people's attention; use illustrations and graphs. This might include anecdotal data (such as stories or testimonials) as well as objective data. Some people are accountants and they really just want a picture with a graph and a bar chart—they want it to look like a stock market report. People absorb information in different ways, so make sure you are communicating your accomplishments in more than one way.

One organization I work with provides eight hundred meals a day to homeless people in New York City; they do this every day of the year. That's close to three hundred thousand meals a year!

A second statistic astounded me as well: the same organization does do all of this for less than $100 a day. Almost everything is donated. Serving nearly three hundred thousand people a year for under $100 a day? That is an outstanding accomplishment, and one that donors would definitely want to know—it's unbelievable.

CASE STATEMENT SECTION 7: VISION

What is your vision of the future? Where is your organization going? In the vision section, tackle some of the fuzzier ideas of the case statement. It's important for the donor to know where your organization is headed. If your goal is to eradicate a certain disease in the developing world, how are you going to do that over the next three-to-five years?

Next, explain how this vision will unfold through your mission and programs. Be specific: Are you going to vaccinate a thousand children a year each year over the next three years? Get even more specific: How will your fundraising efforts help fulfill this vision? Show the relationship between the donor's gift and its impact. Here's an example: "For every ten dollars we receive, we'll be able to vaccinate one child." By directly answering these questions, you'll paint a picture of where the organization is headed in the future, and how your donor or audience can be a part of it. Make it clear that by investing in the current programs, donors pave the way for you to significantly expand your impact. This section is an invitation to envision and create change.

In 1961, President John F. Kennedy stood before Congress and announced that before the end of the decade, the United States would successfully land a man on the moon. At the time, the United States had fallen far behind in the space race with communist Russia. When President Kennedy made this brazen speech, even the greatest scientists were amazed. This endeavor would require an unbelievable amount of money and technology. Kennedy himself once rejected a proposal due to the enormous expense. But with Kennedy's vision of restoring national morale, the United States dedicated $25.8 billion ($257 billion in today's dollars)[3] to this effort. In 1969, with six months to go before the end of the decade, the crew of Apollo 11 made the very first manned moon landing.

Over the last several years I've gotten the chance to work with the Union Rescue Mission in Los Angeles, helping them with an $83 million campaign. The term *skid row* is often used generically to describe poor communities, but Skid Row is an actual place in Los Angeles, a fifty-four-block area officially known as Central City East. The statistics about the homeless population of Los Angeles are hard to wrap my mind around. As of 2021, over fifty thousand people are homeless in the city, with some counts at more than fifty-seven thousand. Skid Row alone is home to thousands. This is probably the greatest human suffering going on in the United States today.

It's overwhelming. What can anyone possibly do to help? (Notice that I didn't include a call to action—just statistics.)

Union Rescue Mission does have a vision for the future. They want to build a new facility in South Los Angeles for women and children that will provide transitional housing for one-third of the nearly one thousand homeless families on Skid Row. When I imagine my wife and children being homeless and realize that this building means hundreds of kids just like my own will no longer be sleeping on the streets, this vision is incredibly compelling. (This is the vision of change—not just the statistics.)

When John F. Kennedy declared that we were going to the moon, he was responding to a climate of fear in the United States, fear that America was falling behind as a nation. Kennedy knew that he needed to cast a bold vision for the country in order to dispel fear and move America forward.

When you communicate a distinct and powerful vision, people will respond. And they will give. So today I'm asking you, What is your short-term dream? Your long-term dream? How are you changing lives? What is your unique vision?

To summarize, the vision section should answer:

- Where are you headed in the future—this year and beyond?

- How will that future vision unfold through your programs?

- How will your fundraising efforts support this vision?

CASE STATEMENT SECTION 8: FINANCIAL NEEDS

In this section of the case statement, you will present your financial needs. This includes all the costs you would expect in a fiscal year, like staffing and payroll, office expenses, program expenses, and what it costs for your organization to exist day to day.

But it is important to describe your financial needs in donor language, using terms that donors will understand. In general, donors are not too interested in itemized budgets of salaries and building utilities and printing costs (although you should certainly have an itemized budget for your own clarity, available to donors if they ask). Instead, describe your budget in terms of programs, since they power the forward movement of your mission. List the money needed to run each component as well as the total financial goal. If you are asking for start-up money, you must show sustainability.

Make sure you do your homework and that your numbers are airtight. You don't want to overestimate or underestimate your financial needs. For example, if you ask for only $100,000 and your actual need turns out to be $150,000, it's hard to go back to a donor and ask for more money. Do the necessary legwork and present your actual need.

CASE STATEMENT SECTION 9: GIFT PLAN

The next section of the case, which is typically on one page, is the gift plan. It's easy to make the mistake of presenting your budget to a potential donor and saying, "Will you please help us?" This is a mistake because it is not specific enough. Remember the second key principle of fundraising: People give because they're asked and shown how. The gift plan is the way of showing how to give through different levels of gifts that together make up the entire budget for an organization. It is not helpful to approach a donor and ask them to just give without showing them how their potential gift fits into the larger plan to fully fund your work.

Several years ago, I received a letter from an individual explaining he was trying to raise $50,000 to build water wells in an African village. It was a compelling cause and I believed in it. But at the end of the letter, he wrote, "Would you help us?" and that was it. My wife and I couldn't write the check for the full $50,000, but we had no idea if he wanted us to give $50, $500, or $5,000. We were left wondering about it. Quite frankly, we gave nothing. We were asked, but we were not shown how. This is where the gift plan comes in. The gift plan is based on our actual prospective donors. It's not a giving pyramid with large gifts and small gifts assigned arbitrarily to various levels; it is based on the people you know and their capacity to give.

With these potential gifts from real people in mind, divide them into three sections—top gifts, middle gifts, and lower gifts. The top gift category consists of people who have the ability to give and a connection with you. They are also generous people. This category should represent at least a third of the money that you need to raise. It will likely come from four to five people, or perhaps 10–20 percent of all your donors.

For example, if we are trying to raise $100,000, the top gift might be $25,000. The next largest gifts, right below that, might be three gifts of $10,000. With just four gifts, including a very significant lead gift, we've covered $55,000 of the $100,000 budget. Again, these levels should be representative of real people on your prospect list.

Moving into the middle level of the gift plan, we may have ten people giving $1,500 each, ten people giving $1,000 each, and twenty people giving $500 each. Then at the lowest level, the gift plan may include forty people each giving $100, and one hundred people who give $25–50. At this point, you are very close to your goal.

By dividing the gifts into top, medium, and lower gift levels, the plan shows how the organization will be funded. Many people would be unable to make that large gift, but when they see how their giving capacity fits into an overall plan, they are very willing to do their part.

Figure 4.4 is an example of a gift plan for the organization Christian Surfers USA. Note the use of the surfboard—not a triangle with arbitrary amounts—integrating their theme into their gift plan!

The three different levels of the surfboard show that this organization is trying to raise $300,000. But it breaks it down into three tiers. The numbers on the left side of the giving plan show how many givers you are seeking at each level (for example, four gifts of $15,000). Just imagine yourself sitting with a donor and saying, "Would you be willing to help us with our organization? Would you be one of these middle givers?" It makes the ask

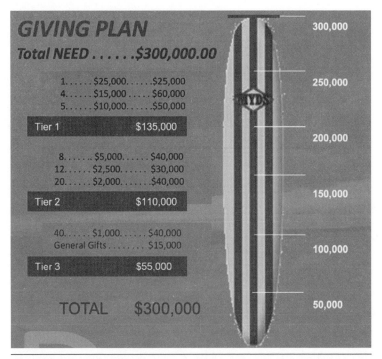

Figure 4.4. Sample gift plan for Christian Surfers organization

much simpler, providing a range for the donor and eliminating the awkwardness and uncertainty of having to ask, "Would you give me a large sum of money?" With the gift plan, the donor can envision how he or she is a vital part of the overall goal.

Figure 4.5 is another gift chart for a field staff person who is raising personal support. You will see her total budget explained at the top of the page, and her plan to raise the $2,350 she needs per month.

As you can see there are different gift levels, but the numbers are much smaller and more appropriate for a person who needs to raise personal support. Imagine sitting with a potential partner and asking them to join your support team and having a simple gift plan like these in front of you and the donor to

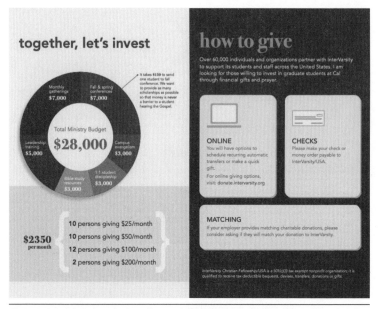

Figure 4.5. Sample gift chart for personal support raising

show them how they can help. *And remember, they do want to help—or they would not be meeting with you!*

It's worth reiterating: the gift plan should be based on real people who are on your priority prospect list, but should also include anticipated gifts from foundations, churches, and businesses if your strategy includes them.

CASE STATEMENT SECTION 10: PROFILE OF LEADERSHIP

The last section of the case is the profile of leadership section. This part of the case statement is where you list all the leaders of your organization: board members, senior staff, noteworthy supporters, and people who just love your organization. You might include members of committees or supporting foundations and corporations.

One organization we've worked with was founded by Billy Graham. Since Billy Graham is incredibly respected by just about everyone in our country, had a great reputation, and had met with every American president for sixty years straight (Truman through Obama),[4] the fact that he was listed as part of their profile of leadership gave this organization a very high level of credibility.

The leadership section does not need to have famous people in it to be effective. I remember meeting with a potential board member for an organization I was leading twenty years ago. As we were looking through the case statement, she got to the profile of leadership page and said, "I know that person! And I know that person! How do I get to be a part of this group?" In this instance, the leadership page worked perfectly—she not only identified the organization as credible because she knew some of the leadership but she also identified herself as a potential leader for the organization. And she did in fact join the board.

Besides listing your leadership, list contact information on this page, including the organization's address, email, phone number, website, Facebook page, Twitter handle, and so on. You might include your nonprofit's IRS tax exempt ID number as well. Make it easy for the donor to get in touch.

A DYNAMIC TOOL

Every one of the ten elements of the case statement is essential. But remember, it's not essential to go through every element in detail when you sit down with a donor. Instead, choose the elements of the case that best relate to that particular donor or prospect. Remember the case statement can be used both horizontally and vertically.

As your organization grows and changes each year, your case statement will grow too. Every nonprofit needs a clear way to communicate their organization or they will flounder. Each year, organizations should revise their case statement; it is updated to reflect the gradual changes that occur in the life of an organization.

Ultimately, creating and using the case statement enables prospective donors to get a real inside look at your organization, a vital part of taking your donors seriously.

To download sample case statements and other resources, go to TheFocusGroup.com/partners.

PRACTICE 2

LEADERSHIP

Several years ago, one of my friends felt a calling to become a missionary in the Dominican Republic. She was a person who grew up in the church, but she did not have an extensive network of people to rely on to fund her work. She did have a few close friends who believed in her and believed in the work that she was being called to do, so she asked her close friends to form a team around her and help her with fundraising. She asked these friends to not only give their own gift but share the vision of the work with two or three others they knew who could also give similar gifts. That team worked together, and in a few short months my friend raised all the funds she needed to launch. The team continued to function for the entire time she was in the mission field—almost ten years! My friend had formed what I refer to as a Taking Donors Seriously team (TDS team).

Fundamentally, you can't take donors seriously without serious leadership. Remember, people give to people they know and trust. Your leadership carries the vision of your organization to the donors, connecting your prospects with the case and inviting them to be part of the vision. Leadership should be from two sources: staff and volunteers. Together they perform seven essential functions of leadership:

1. Prayer
2. Preparing Materials
3. Donor Research
4. Being a Caller/Asker
5. Events and Communication
6. Strategy Management
7. Data Management

No matter the size of your organization, whether it's huge or just one person on staff, having a TDS team is vital to your fundraising success.

I want to emphasize that this TDS team is different from your board or fundraising subcommittee of the board. The TDS team is responsible for asking and thanking major donors. These major donors may be few in number, but they are the lifeblood of your organization.

Now let's get specific about each function of leadership. Once you know how each component contributes to your TDS team, you'll have a better idea of who you need to recruit to your team.

LEADERSHIP FUNCTION 1: PRAYER

The first Young Life club was started by Jim Rayburn in 1939, but in reality, Young Life had begun six years earlier with a prayer meeting across the street from Gainesville High School (Texas). In Rayburn's own words:

> I found out that across the street from the high school a group of elderly women had been meeting for six years, every Monday morning, getting down on their knees in

the living room of dear old Mrs. Frasher. They prayed every Monday morning for six years, long before I ever heard of Gainesville, Texas, for the high school kids across the street. I was there a year before I heard of that prayer meeting. I used to go over there with those five or six old ladies and get down on my knees with them after that club started to roll. That was the thing the Lord used to start it. Back in seminary (at Dallas Theological Seminary), a group of kids going to school there got interested in this club and started to pray. They'd meet every Monday night and pray while I went to the club meeting in Gainesville. It's no wonder we had a revival in that school![1]

Prayer remains one of the most critical ingredients in ministries' successes, and it is the first function of leadership for fundraising.

As part of forming a TDS team, develop an intentional strategy of praying for both the work your organization is doing and for the donors who are partnering with you to make this work possible. A prayer strategy is more than just opening and closing your TDS team meeting with prayer. It is a commitment to creating a strategy, even recruiting someone on your TDS team who commits to gather and distribute prayer requests or organize quarterly prayer times on your behalf. A staff person can do this, but if you believe in the power of prayer, then why not create an intentional strategy around such an important activity.

LEADERSHIP FUNCTION 2: PREPARING MATERIALS

The second function of leadership on your TDS team is preparing materials, including the case statement. This role is best carried out by a staff person, since they will have access to things like the logo, photos, and stories of lives that have been recently impacted by the organization.

When your TDS team begins to meet, the staff person will bring a completed draft of the case to the meeting for the group to review and give feedback. This person may also need to prepare additional support materials for fundraising, such as pledge cards.

LEADERSHIP FUNCTION 3: DONOR RESEARCH

The third function of leadership is donor research. This means preparing background information on your prospects. The staff and a few key volunteers can help provide this necessary background information.

It's essential to know each prospective donor's history with your organization. Have they given consistently in the past? What programs are they passionate about?

In order to take donors seriously, it is critical to have a general sense of each prospect to determine where each fits in the fundraising strategy, as well as an appropriate range of giving to ask them to consider. Do you know this person's capacity for giving? Do you have a general sense of their financial background?

Most importantly, you want to know about the donors themselves: Why is this cause near and dear to their hearts? What are their stories? Who got them involved in the first place? You want to be able to engage the donor through the person who knows them best, around an opportunity that they care about the most.

Recently while I was serving on a TDS committee for an organization I volunteer with, we discussed a major donor who has a history with our organization. We were brainstorming the best way to thank this person for their gift. We knew their family has a child with special needs, so we asked the director of our special needs program to take time to call them and thank them for their recent gift. It was a small gesture, but hopefully a meaningful one. Our simple brainstorming was an example of doing the research on how to best engage that donor.

LEADERSHIP FUNCTION 4: BEING A CALLER/ASKER

The fourth function of leadership is to be a caller, or asker. This is the person who actually asks for the gift and invites the prospect to engage with your organization as a way to thank them. Callers can be both staff and volunteers. In many organizations, only staff serve as callers. This is a mistake, because we want to engage the prospective donors with the person who knows them best, which might be a staff person or a volunteer. We always want to have the person that knows the donor the best be the primary person to engage with the donor.

The most important step is getting the meeting. Who is the easiest person to say yes to and hardest to say no to? The person who knows you the best. If my mom calls me and asks me to meet with her for just about anything, I'm going to say yes. Designate the person with the best connection to the donor as that person's assigned caller.

People who are callers should be giving sacrificially to your organization too. They need to be able to say to your prospects, "Will you join me in supporting this organization?" In my experience, people who are not themselves donors do *not* make good askers.

How do you find these callers? We'll tackle that in a moment.

LEADERSHIP FUNCTION 5:
EVENTS AND COMMUNICATION

The fifth function of leadership for a TDS team is to work on events and communication. While the TDS team as a whole is not responsible for managing the details and putting on events, they are responsible for coordinating the overall plan and strategy of engaging donors. The TDS team speaks into the timing of the events and communications. The timing of an annual banquet can affect your major donor strategy, so the TDS team needs to have a bird's eye view of the overall plan.

LEADERSHIP FUNCTION 6:
STRATEGY MANAGEMENT

The sixth function of the leadership is strategy management. The strategy manager, who is a member of the TDS team, keeps you focused on doing the right things at the right time. They keep the fundraising "train" on the right track, leaving the station on time and headed in the right direction.

You might be surprised to learn that we recommend that the strategy manager be a volunteer, not a staff person. When a volunteer steps into this role, a whole new level of ownership is shared within an organization. Remember the principle we presented earlier: people give when they are involved and have a sense of ownership. The strategy manager functions as the chairperson of the TDS team. By default that leadership role will fall to a staff person unless there is an intentional effort to involve someone else.

Many of you may stop and say, "Well, I have no idea who this could be. A person who would help me with fundraising and wants to perform the strategy manager role. There is no one I know who would do this." More than likely, you already know this person. He or she is already a major donor to your work, probably owns their own business (or used to), and is a well-respected member of the community. You are not asking this person to help you run a banquet or golf tournament but asking them to use their gifts in a very strategic way.

At first glance it may seem that finding this person would not be necessary or even appropriate if you are raising personal support as a missionary or field staff worker, but the opposite is true—it is even more important to have this person if you are a missionary or field staff worker. Most missionaries and field staff workers are doing work away from their "home network," which makes ongoing communication and donor cultivation much harder. When you form a TDS team and recruit a strategy manager to help lead your major donor work, you are gaining help in an area that is desperately needed, since most support from home networks wanes over time without proper care and cultivation.

To function effectively, the strategy manager must have access to the priority prospect list and all relevant data. The data should be in a format that allows them to look one week, one month, or a year ahead of time to see what needs to happen.

LEADERSHIP FUNCTION 7: DATA MANAGEMENT

The last person or function you need to recruit is that of a data manager. Now this person may be the easiest to find—it's someone who loves your organization and loves numbers. Sometimes this person is also a primary caller but not always. Regardless, they love their calculator and numbers make sense to them—but they absolutely must be a donor themselves.

The data manager's job is to keep track of all of the day-to-day details—your asks, your thank-yous, and any other data that you need to be tracking. They know who has given what and who is falling behind in their pledges.

The data manager also makes sure every prospective donor is listed on the prospect list and is evaluated in terms of priority level, target range of giving, and the designated contact person/point of request. A well-constructed priority prospect list (PPL) will serve as an effective, dependable guide in your fundraising process. It is impossible to devise a solid fundraising strategy without a complete and accurate PPL. And without a reliable strategy, it's impossible to devise a realistic plan.

The data manager also serves as a check and balance to the TDS chairperson (the strategy manager). By providing and tracking accurate data, this person provides critical leadership on your TDS team.

THE EXECUTIVE DIRECTOR AS CHIEF FUNDRAISER

In a nonprofit organization, what role does the executive director play on the TDS team? My friend Dr. Jay Barber, former president of Warner Pacific College, sums it up this way: "Executive directors need to stay close to the major donors."

It is so tempting for the executive director to delegate fundraising to the development department or the director of development (if your organization has one). But the task of working with major donors cannot be delegated completely. Of course, some of the tasks of fundraising can be delegated, but not the relational touch points.

The executive director needs to communicate the same message to all donors within an organization. The only thing that changes is the delivery method. We will discuss this in chapter eight, but imagine that an executive director shares the impact of a gift in a face-to-face meeting with a major donor, in a small group setting with mid-level donors, and through a letter with smaller donors; at each meeting the executive director shared the same message, only the delivery method changed.

No matter how small or large an organization, the bottom line is that executive directors must take on a leadership role in fundraising. If you are a field worker or a missionary, you are the executive director.

There are three primary roles that the executive director should play in fundraising:

- Contribute to creating the messaging for the case statement.

- Have a role in maintaining a relationship with the top ten to twelve donors.

- Partner with the strategy manager to build the teams that will give leadership to all the strategies and events.

Depending on the size of your organization you may or may not have a full-time development director. That's okay. Remember, one of the reasons that we recommend having a volunteer serve as the strategy manager is that we want there to be a strong sense of shared ownership—community around the mission you are a part of.

PARTNERING WITH BOARD MEMBERS AND VOLUNTEERS

How do you maximize the involvement of your board members? We've developed these guidelines to help your board members become your partners in fundraising:

- Ask a select group of board members dedicated to working with major donors to be on the TDS team. The key is to select a capable TDS chairperson to serve as the strategy manager who has the respect of his or her peers and has the capacity to make a major gift.

- With the assistance of the TDS chair, carefully recruit the TDS committee members. Typically, only about a third of any board is capable and willing to be involved in direct donor asks. It is better to have a smaller committee of willing and capable members than a larger group where everyone doesn't share the load. Remember, volunteers can also function as callers.

- Prepare a TDS committee job description outlining each member's responsibilities. Be sure to discuss how to handle confidential donor information.

- Provide opportunities for training in how to make calls to key donors. Provide resources for accurate contact information and appropriate background information.

- Set realistic goals about how many people to contact and how much gift income to bring in.

- Establish procedures in advance for reporting, accountability, and transparency between team members and with the full board.

- Appropriately recognize and thank board members for their leadership in this key area.

FINDING CALLERS

One question I frequently hear during TDS trainings is, "Where do we find people to be the TDS callers?" The first place to look is your board, as we discussed above. The second place to look is your list of current donors. Look for major donors who already demonstrate they believe in the organization and its mission. By inviting them to be callers for your organization, you are helping to convert them from the transaction of giving you money into a partner with you in advancing the kingdom of God.

A caller should be someone who is involved and has already made a financial commitment to your organization. If someone says, "I want to ask people for money, but I don't want to give any money myself," you should probably tell them, "Thanks, but no thanks" or "Maybe you'd like to help us with our fundraising events."

Frankly, your callers should be people who are inviting their friends to join in doing what they are already doing. Recently I was with a major donor who was offering to give a large gift to an organization. In his enthusiasm for giving, he said, "I'm not only going to give this gift, but I'm also going to get all my best friends who I play golf with each week to give just as much." This is the kind of person who could serve as a very effective caller for the organization.

Often, great TDS callers will own their own businesses. The key is to find people who recognize the significance of relationships and will stay committed over time.

Good fundraising flows out of relationship-building by your TDS team—which, remember, is made up of staff and volunteers. Make sure to choose quality and tenacity over quantity. In other words, don't ask callers to be responsible for more than five donors and prospects. Three to five prospective donors will be plenty for a TDS member to be responsible for.

START MEETING AND DON'T STOP

When discussing the functions of the TDS team, I am often asked, "How do I get started?"

In 1994, I had the opportunity to start my first TDS team. I learned there is a secret to starting a team. The secret is to just keep meeting and never stop. Go ahead and set up the first meeting; then keep meeting regularly. But you will say, "Wait. I don't have my strategy manager yet. All I have is my accountant who has agreed to be my data manager." The truth is that you do have a team now—there are two of you, and you should start meeting. Set a date, perhaps the first Tuesday of every month. Now you and your accountant are going to have lunch together. I even suggest that if you're the staff person, take the initiative and offer to bring lunch. Meet the first time and just keep meeting on your designated day and time.

Why does this work? Because momentum is created by your commitment to meet as a team. Slowly you will interact with other people and invite them into this group that meets at your designated time. You will begin to get a sense of other people's gifts by getting to know them. And you will start to gain momentum.

When I first started my team in 1994, we would sit around, eat Subway sandwiches, and talk about the TDS principles. We would often set goals for ourselves—and completely miss the deadlines we set. But then we would keep trying, and after a year we had fully implemented TDS. We were no longer struggling to raise our budget.

I live in Florida, so I have to play a certain amount of golf. I'm not very good at it though. One morning, as I swung and managed to move the ball only a few inches, my optimistic partner said, "Well, Brad, at least you're advancing the ball." Sometimes that's all we can do. So advance the ball by finding your leaders and meeting with them regularly. Even if you have a frustrating meeting or two where you feel like you're not gaining traction, getting ready to meet with your key leaders and meeting regularly with them advances the ball in ways that might not be immediately visible.

It can be daunting at first to form a TDS team, but if you invite people in and ask them to serve in a specific role that they are gifted and willing to do, you will find that fundraising becomes much, much easier.

A $25 MILLION TDS TEAM

Several years ago, I worked with one of our clients to raise about $50 million. As a part of this campaign we helped them launch an executive campaign committee (ECC). An ECC is a concept The FOCUS Group developed in which a group of major donors commit to giving lead gifts to a campaign and agree to invite a few of their friends to join them in giving at that level. The FOCUS Group works very hard to create this committee for the capital campaigns we are involved with, but an ECC is just a TDS team with a bigger goal.

On this occasion, there was a billionaire who had agreed to serve on the ECC. What was even more amazing was that this billionaire had committed to giving over a million dollars and had offered to host the ECC meeting at his vacation home. Now, I often interact with wealthy people, but I don't typically get invited to the vacation homes of billionaires. According to *Forbes*, there are only 735 billionaires in the United States—so this was a special event.[2] Upon arriving at the billionaire's home for the ECC meeting, I was greeted by not one, but two layers of security. When I finally made it to the door, I was welcomed by the billionaire himself. He knew my name, although we had never met (clearly there was some system going on with the security officers!).

Over the next thirty minutes, all of the other guests arrived, and we milled around for a casual social hour. Then a person came out of the kitchen and rang a bell, announcing that dinner was served; we would continue our conversations over dinner. As the guests walked into the dining room, I was directed to eat in the kitchen. I suddenly felt like I was on *Downton Abbey*, and I was one of the house servants. Didn't the host realize who I was—a fundraising consultant?!

My story is such a clear reminder of the many leadership roles in a campaign. Even though I would like to think of myself as an important contact for that billionaire, I'm not. As a fundraising consultant, I wasn't needed at the dining room table. Instead, my job was to help my client get the right people around that table and be sure that the right topics were covered. I had done that, and the president of my client's organization was there at the table, fully prepared for that conversation.

The fundraising process requires many types of leadership. I desperately wanted that client to be successful, and the best way I could do that was to facilitate a meeting that I ultimately didn't sit in on. As you think about your own role in fundraising, and as you seek to take your donors seriously, ask yourself what your role is. Are you a staff person? Are you a caller? A volunteer? Are you called to set the table or make it possible for others to eat at that table?

In the end, my client successfully met and exceeded the $50 million goal for their campaign. Those folks sitting around the dining room table gave or helped raise over 50 percent of the funds given to the campaign. It was a highly successful evening, despite the fact I was eating in the kitchen.

Whatever your role is, embrace it and enjoy it. And don't worry if you find yourself in the kitchen!

PRACTICE 3
PROSPECTS

Over the last thirty years, working with hundreds of non-profits has allowed me to observe a consistent trend: most organizations allow 50 percent or more of their donors to lapse on an annual basis. A small portion of that has to do with timing—a donor may give in December of one year, and then thirteen months later give a gift in January—but the majority of lapsed donors are just that, lapsed.

One organization had more than one million donors give to their cause over a twenty-year period, but in the current year, only one hundred thousand of those million were giving. They had allowed nine hundred thousand donors—a full 90 percent—to lapse. That organization had a pretty bad "back door" problem. They were doing a good job bringing donors in the front door, but they were losing them by neglecting to follow up, thank them, and stay connected to them.

Perhaps you are saying, "I couldn't imagine having a problem like that. Who was that organization?" But when you make a list of current and former donors, your statistics aren't all that better. I have surveyed dozens of nonprofits, and regardless of the type of organization, they typically have a history of losing 50 percent of their donors on a year-to-year basis.

So why does this happen? It is much harder to find a new donor than to keep an existing one. After all, donors have already demonstrated that they believe in our mission. So why are organizations prone to search for the new donor while neglecting the donors they have? I believe this happens because organizations haven't created a plan for taking care of their donors.

Once you create a strategy for staying in touch with each person, you will schedule these folks into your calendar and keep growing the relationships. Like a fruit tree, you may not see much fruit the first year; but by year six, your tree will be bearing more fruit than you can eat. Don't drop your donors. They may have wandered off and gotten caught up in their own lives. It's up to you to keep nurturing the relationship and keep it strong. It is much harder to find a new donor than to keep an existing one. Keep this in mind as you identify prospects.

FINDING NEW DONORS

One of the most frequent questions I get is, "Can you help me find new donors?" This question seems to weigh on every fundraiser's mind. There's a powerful myth in the fundraising world that the solution to all your fundraising problems is finding more donors. The real solution is being a good steward of the donors you already have. But assuming you have never raised money before, and you are just starting out as a new fundraiser, you do need a method of identifying who to ask.

Step One. Start by making a list of one hundred potential donors based on the following five questions.

First, who are the people that have a close relationship with you? Who are the people who believe in you? It's okay to put your mom, your nieces, your cousins, and your grandparents on this list. You might be saying, "Oh, I can't put my mom on the list because . . ." Don't make decisions for other people. The question is not, "Who loves you and thinks you should do this?" but "Who loves you?" Also remember at this point you are just making a list, not asking—so instead of excluding anyone, just list out everyone, including family members, that loves you.

Second, who are the people that you know who love the ethos or core of your organization? If you are raising money for an organization for animals, ask yourself, "Who's a cat lover? Who has rescued shelter animals before?"

Third, who do you know that loves your specific organization? This could even be your current executive director or current board chair.

Fourth, who do you know that has a giving spirit? Think about the people who have given you things when you haven't asked. Who is the one friend who takes the time to buy you a gift or card for your birthday? Who is always making cookies for other people? Who always remembers you? These are examples of demonstrated generosity that don't necessarily have to do with actual money.

Fifth, who do you know that has the financial capacity to give? There are a lot of people in the world who are incredibly generous, and they may know you really well. However, if these people are your college roommates and they're in their early twenties, they probably don't have a lot of money. We want to focus on people at different stages in their lives and give them opportunities to be involved in ways that work for them. You can often observe wealth through people's lifestyles. Do they have a large house or a vacation home? Do they own their own business? Take exotic vacations? Give philanthropically? Have affiliations with nonprofits or foundations? Send their children to private schools?

Remember, the ability to give is in no way related to the desire to give. There are many people with modest financial ability who give with all their heart and as much as they can. And some rich people don't have the gift of giving.

The goal is to start with a list of one hundred people, and not to make their decisions for them. You may start thinking of people and then say, "Oh, that person won't want to support me, because of x, y, z." Nonetheless, stop editing and stop making decisions for other people, and just make a list of one hundred people.

Step two. Then using the five questions above, assess how many of the five attributes each of the people on your list has. If a person is a yes to all five (they know you, love the work your organization does, love your organization, have demonstrated generosity, and have the capacity to give a large gift) then you should be pursuing them as a top prospect. However, if the opposite is true and they have only one of the five, then spend more time building a relationship with them over time. You may consider them a potential donor to your organization in the near future. People with these attributes often make good middle-level donors.

BUILDING DEEPER RELATIONSHIPS WITH DONORS

How do you build these relationships? You don't want to simply approach a potential donor and resolve to build a relationship with them. Start with what you know:

- How did the donor get involved with your organization?
- Who in your organization does the donor have the best relationship with?
- What in your organization is the donor most interested in?

It is much better to start with some basis for the relationship. You want to identify who should encourage the donor's financial support over the long term. Is the prospective donor's son-in-law already involved as a volunteer in the organization? Has this donor already connected with the community you are trying to serve in some other way?

In all your contact with donors, keep listening. Use what they tell you to nurture and define the relationship. If you take them seriously, stay with them over time, and listen to them carefully, you will invariably find the relationship changing and almost always growing.

Your donors are spread across a wide relational continuum. Some are into analytics and others are interested in hearing stories of others' lives. Some of them may be open to a lot of contact and a close relationship with you and some may want a few modest touch points per year. No two donors are the same, and if you truly want to take donors seriously, you will spend the time to understand what is important to the specific donor you are engaged with.

One of the ways I have learned to identify what "type" of a relationship a donor wants to engage in is how they respond to the invitation to connect. When you ask if the donor would be willing to meet with you for an update about your work, or to talk to them about a gift, where do they suggest that you meet? A Zoom call is better than a phone call; but a coffee meeting is better than a Zoom meeting; but an invitation to visit with someone in the evening for dinner is better than a coffee meeting. The most intimate place a donor can invite you to meet, I have learned, is their vacation home. When a donor invites you to meet with them at their vacation home, they are inviting you into a place that is sacred to them, and they are telling you about the level of commitment they have toward your organization.

In a relationally driven fundraising effort, you need to consistently ask yourself, *Who is the donor? Who am I to this donor?* and *What does our organization mean to the donor?* If you are faithful over time in this regard, even distant relationships will develop as you build trust, resulting in more active contact and involvement with you and your organization. But remember, no two donors are the same!

PRIORITIZING (ORGANIZING) PROSPECTS

When we talk about prioritizing our prospects, we are talking about organizing our donors and prioritizing our time and energy. Now that you have made a list of the donors who currently give to you, have recently given to you, or who may give to you in the future, how do you approach them? You probably don't have a million donors, but even managing a hundred potential donors means you need to figure out how to prioritize. Remember, taking every donor seriously does not mean treating every donor the same.

Each donor and prospect should be assigned to one of the four levels below. Each priority level has a different strategy for how to approach the donor. Make sure to note the priority level on your spreadsheet as you move through your list.

Priority 1 donors are people who are accessible and available for meetings. They are people you already know well, with whom you have cultivated a close relationship. They also have the capacity to give 2.5 percent or more of your fundraising goal, whether your organization has a budget of $100,000 or $1 million. These donors are people who are giving big gifts relative to your budget.

If you need to raise $100,000 a year, then a Priority 1 donor would be someone who could give you $2,500 or more. You might have someone on your list who has given you only $100. But if they have the potential to give a much larger gift, then call them a Priority 1, even though they have not yet given at that level. Make sure to segment your list based on what someone *could give* rather than what they *have given* in the past.

Because there are a limited number of Priority 1 donors, the work you will do with these donors primarily takes place face-to-face and is managed by your TDS team.

Priority 2 donors are people who have many of the same characteristics as Priority 1—they are people you know well, with whom you have cultivated a close relationship. The difference is that for whatever reason, they don't have the financial capacity to give as much money as the Priority 1 donors. Priority 2 donors have the ability to give between 0.5 percent and 2.5 percent of your fundraising goal. With a $100,000 budget, these donors have the capacity to give you a gift between $500 and $2,500. There are certainly more people in this category. But again, these are people you are closely connected to who are available for meetings.

Since Priority 2 donors will be greater in number, you will sometimes cultivate them in face-to-face meetings, but you will also use small groups and phone or Zoom calls to cultivate these donors. Priority 2 donors are also managed by your TDS team.

Priority 3 donors have the capacity to give you 0.5 percent of your budget or less. For whatever reason, they can't give as large of a gift. Based on a $100,000 budget, these folks could give you a gift of $500 or less per year.

This group of people should be pursued through events or other large group-based solicitation strategies such as mail, giving days, or other fundraisers. Priority 3 donors are not managed by the TDS team, but by staff or special committees to engage smaller donors, usually through events.

Priority 4 donors are really important prospects that we think could be Priority 1 or Priority 2. However, we don't know them well enough yet to be able to determine their interest or connection to our organization.

When someone tells you about a person that they think could help you with your organization, make them a Priority 4. Then see what you can learn from other people who may know them to determine if they would be a good prospect for your organization.

Because we all have limited time and resources, we must segment and prioritize our donors. We want to focus the most time and energy on the group of donors that can give us the most money and do the most good for our organization.

Please note: some people are giving generously and sacrificially, but their giving capacity makes them a Priority 3 prospect. You should know your donors well enough that if a person is giving on that level, but they are giving to you sacrificially, then treat them like they're a Priority 1 donor. Why? Because this honors their sacrifices and honors God, recalling the widow's mite story in Luke 21.

I remember a woman who used to support an organization I was involved in. She worked two jobs, she was a single mom, she had three kids, and every month she sent our organization a check for fifty dollars. That fifty dollars was way more money to her than the five thousand dollars from our top giver. We knew her well enough to know that fifty dollars was a big deal, so we tended that relationship with more time and care. It's important to honor people's hearts and their intent in their giving.

TELLING EVERY KID

A friend of mine, Mary, was a new field staff person for a parachurch ministry, and she needed to raise a very large sum. She went through this same process of identifying one hundred people and came up with a woman, Esther, who had a giving spirit (number 4) and had the financial capacity to give (number 5); the only thing she didn't know was whether there was a real connection there (numbers 1, 2, or 3—love for Mary, the cause, or the organization).

Mary went to visit Esther and spent time with her, explaining what they were trying to do in their community. She shared her organization's vision, and at the end of their time together, she asked her if she would be willing to make a gift. This gift would help them start the ministry at a particular school.

Esther's response was to ask, "Do you tell every kid that God loves them?" Mary said, "Yes, and we also invite them to camp, and we take them to weekly meetings and have these programs that we go through, and there are sporting events and . . ."

Esther stopped her and looked at her and asked, "Do you tell every kid that God loves them?" Mary once again said yes, but then went on to describe more about their programs.

Esther stopped her again and said, "I'll give you the money if you tell every kid that God loves them." Mary said, "Well, ma'am, we do tell every kid that God loves them." And then Esther said, "Well, I'm going to support you."

Esther's repeated question answered question number 2— she loved the cause of the organization even though she did not know the staff person or the organization. She had three out of the five attributes of a good donor for that organization.

Sometimes sitting down and getting to know people allows us to discover their deep connection to the ethos of our organization. When we interact with donors, we are often quick to offer up stories about our organization. We want to share stories of the people we are impacting or talk about how amazing our new program is. But in our eagerness to share, we often forget to ask questions and learn the stories of the person who is sitting right in front of us. We all have stories. There is a reason that your donors are currently giving or potentially interested in supporting your work. Do you know what it is?

As you interact with donors today, I challenge you to pause and ask your existing donors two simple questions: "What are some other organizations you support?" and "What part of our work are you most excited about, and why?"

MANAGING PROSPECTS

By now you should have a list with all your donors and prospects (or a list of a hundred potential donors if you are just getting started), and you are beginning to understand that each donor has a priority level.

Keeping track of this data will help you effectively reach your donors.

Prospect management entails collecting all the data you need to keep track of and keeping it one place. By the end of this chapter, you will have created a priority prospect list (PPL), like the sample in table 6.1. Again, you can manage this data in a spreadsheet, or if you want, using The FOCUS Group's Windshield 2020® software. If you are using a spreadsheet, each question should have its own column to record the data. However you manage your data, the concepts presented in this chapter must be components of your donor database. They are simple but powerful when applied correctly.

Table 6.1. Priority prospect list (PPL)

Name(s)	Type	Attributes	Priority #	Strategy	Primary Caller	Follow-Up/ Next Steps
Bob and Michelle Smith	Individual	Board member	1	Individual	Sharon Davis	
Kimberly Thompson	Individual	Alumni	3	Group	Rachel Williams	
Trinity Baptist	Church	Former staff	2	Group	Blake Miller	

DONOR TYPE

First, what type of prospect are they? An individual, a foundation, a church, a business? Clarifying this is critical to managing prospects so you can filter your prospects by donor type, which allows you to develop different strategies for different types of donors.

ATTRIBUTES

Second, what attributes apply to your prospect? For example, if your prospect is an individual, is this person a volunteer? A current board member? A former board member? A close friend of the president? Are their kids involved in your organization? Those are attributes you should record in this column.

PRIORITY NUMBER

Next, if you haven't already, you need to keep track of the priority level of each donor. Remember, Priority 1 is for people who have the ability to give 2.5 percent or more of your fundraising need (and are already close connections); Priority 2 people have the ability to give 0.5–2.5 percent of your fundraising need (and are also already connected to you); Priority 3 donors have the ability to give less than 0.5 percent of your fundraising need; and Priority 4 donors could be a Priority 1 or 2, but you don't know them well enough to give them a financial rating.

STRATEGY

Fourth, you'll need to gather data about the best strategy for reaching this prospect. What is the best way to ask them for a gift? Group fundraising events are a very efficient way to raise money, but less effective relative to the amount raised, compared to individual meetings. Then again, we don't have time to meet with everyone individually. You will need to answer the best way to reach them, given the balance you are trying to strike between efficient and effective fundraising. Ultimately there are two fundamental strategies, group or individual, but then you want to narrow it even further. Do you hope this person attends your golf tournament? Would this prospect be more inclined to attend your banquet?

CALLER

The fifth thing you want to keep track of is the caller. The caller is the person who has the primary relationship with the donors. Since "people give to people they know and trust," the caller needs to be the person who knows the donor best. Ultimately, the caller is responsible for asking and thanking the donors; the caller manages the relationship.

NEXT STEPS

Next Steps and Follow-Up Steps is a place to record the next step of getting in touch with this donor or cultivating the relationship. Are you meeting for coffee on Thursday to share more about your mission? Write that down here. Do you need to present your case statement? Or is the next step you asking them for a gift?

ESTIMATING AND KEEPING TRACK OF FINANCIAL GIFTS

Finally, you will want to record data that reflects the actual financial capacity of each donor, as seen in table 6.2. You need to determine the target high and target low for each donor.

Table 6.2. Financial capacity data

Name(s)	Target High	Target Low	Asked For	Committed	Last Year's Giving
Bob and Michelle Smith	–	–	$25,000	–	$12,000
Kimberly Thompson	$500	$200	–	–	$200
Trinity Baptist	–	–	–	$1,500	

TARGET HIGH

You may be thinking, *How do I know what a target high is for a prospect?* Well, it's a pretty simple answer: What is the most you are willing to ask them for, based on everything you know about them? Determine what you are willing to ask them for based on your relationship with them, everything you know about them, your research, and their prior giving.

Others may suggest that you ask people for a huge gift because you don't want to leave money on the table. But remember, fundraising is long-term, relational work. We don't mind leaving money on the table because we are not leaving the table.

TARGET LOW

How do you know what the target low is? There are two ways. One, it's based on what they gave you last year. Or, two, if they didn't give you anything last year, what are you 90 percent or more sure that they will give you this year?

ASKED FOR

Once you have asked, record the amount that was asked for or was committed. Once a person has committed an amount of money, record that data as well.

COMMITTED

This is simply the number that the donor told you they would commit to give to your organization this year.

SUMMARY

The numbers in the Target Amounts and the Asked For columns are in motion. That is, they move from left to right until they reach the Committed column. When you ask for a certain amount, it should be recorded in the Asked For column, and immediately the amounts in the Target High and Target Low columns should be removed. When the donor commits to giving, the amount in the Asked For column should be removed, and the amount committed should be recorded in the Committed column.

For each donor, there will usually be an active dollar amount in only one of these three areas: the Target High/Target Low columns, the Asked For column, or the Committed column. However, a donor may commit to a specific amount and indicate that an additional gift may be given before the end of the year. In that case, this donor would have an amount in the Committed column, and projected amounts in the Target High/Target Low columns.

When you have completed projections for all your donors and prospects, the Target High and Asked For and Committed totals combined should be one and one-half times your goal:

Target High total + Asked For total + Committed total = 1.5 × the Fundraising Goal

The total Target Low, when added to the Asked For and Committed totals, should equal or exceed your goal:

Target Low total + Asked For total + Committed total = Fundraising goal (or more!)

Your numbers should always be somewhat conservative, so do not arbitrarily adjust your numbers upward just to make the totals work. When the potential and committed numbers do meet the established parameters, the task that remains is to follow through with donors, finalizing their commitments and then monitoring the receipt of gifts during the rest of the year.

The data we have about our prospects helps us project where we're going. At The FOCUS Group, we've developed our own software called Windshield 2020. It's not Customer Relationship Management (CRM) like Salesforce or Raiser's Edge; tools like those focus on what has happened in the past. What we've developed in Windshield 2020 is a way of looking at the key information to have perfect 20/20 vision about your fundraising future. You can map out the same data using Excel or a legal pad, but we've developed this software that tracks it perfectly.

To review, these are the key pieces of data that you need to manage prospects and plan how to approach them:

- Name(s)
- Donor Type
- Donor Attributes
- Donor Priority
- Solicitation Strategy
- Primary Caller
- Financial Projections (Target Low, Target High, Asked For, Committed)

Remember that organization that had a million donors? When I did a deeper dive into their data, I discovered that of the 900,000 lapsed donors, fewer than 3,500 of those people had given over $10,000. While it may seem daunting to determine the key pieces of data for 900,000 donors, it was incredibly helpful to find out that by pursuing less than 1 percent of the people who were lapsed donors, they could recover the gifts from the people that had made the largest gifts to the organization.

Gathering all this information can be hard work! But managing prospect data is key to raising all the funds you need for your organization.

PRACTICE 4
THE STRATEGY

When I was a new, young executive director of a small nonprofit in St. Augustine, I was living in two fundraising worlds. I was doing what I saw in the world by doing transactional fundraising while simultaneously implementing the fundraising methods contained in this book. The organization I was leading was planning events haphazardly while pursuing people relationally. One year we decided that a great idea it would be to have a hoedown. We would have a country-western band, a barbecue, and an auction. We rented a hall, hired a band, and gave a caterer a large deposit. As the date of the event approached, it was clear that we were not selling enough tickets and had not received enough auction items. I called an emergency board meeting and pressured our board to "get to work." One of the board members, who was in his eighties, said that he was sorry but he could not attend due to the fact he could not drive at night. Before the end of the board meeting, my eighty-year-old board member grabbed an extra case statement to share with one of his friends, and the rest of the board went out trying to make our hoedown a success.

Fast forward a couple of weeks, after the hoedown happened. We did not lose money but only made a few thousand dollars. I will never forget the call I got from my eighty-year-old board member the day after the event. He called to ask me how the event went, and to inform me that he shared the case statement with one of his friends and his friend had given him a check for our organization for $5,000! That eighty-year-old board member was strategic in his thinking and invited one of his friends to join him in supporting our organization, whereas the rest of us worked hard to get people to come to our hoedown.

Over the years I have heard hundreds of ideas about the next best fundraiser. Thousands of hours have been spent putting on events that could have been devoted to building relationships. Events have an important role in an overall fundraising plan, but they are not the centerpiece of a robust fundraising strategy. You need to invest your time, effort, and resources to work on building a strategy to develop genuine friendship because that's what donors are: friends. Remember, people give to people they know and trust—not only to causes. Friendship is what it's all about. You'll get occasional small donations from people who attend your fundraisers, but this is not the most effective way to reach your goal.

You need to be building long-term relationships, not collecting money. You need a partner, not a donation! Until you understand this idea deeply and apply it consistently to your cause, fundraising will always trouble you.

Efficient and effective also means realistic. I have been part of many fundraising committees that just want to send a letter to the one person who they know can afford to fund the whole project. Or they want to send a letter asking everybody for money and then wait for the money to come in.

Events can be incredibly appealing and may appear to be a shortcut to your goal, but which feels better—building relationship with someone and asking them to partner with you in advancing your cause by becoming a monthly partner at $100 per month, or asking someone to buy a $100 raffle ticket for something they don't want or need?

It's not just events that are the problem. Over the last thirty years, dozens of people have told me that their fundraising solution is to ask so many number of people to each give the same amount: "I need to raise $100,000, so I will ask one hundred people to give $1,000." This is what I call "fundraising multiplication tables," and it simply does not work. Good giving must be variable. After all, the humans that are doing the giving are also varied and variable. When you ask all your donors for the same amount, the person who could give ten times that amount winds up giving you a much smaller amount; the person who was never going to give you anything still gives you nothing. The math is correct, but only on paper. Meanwhile, you wind up with a failed fundraising campaign.

Several years ago, I was working with an executive director of an amazing organization. He had become convinced that he could solve his fundraising problems by asking all the alumni of his organization to become a "partner" for $5 a month. He was convinced that if he did this, the partner giving would sustain the organization long into the future. He spent a significant amount of time preparing to launch the new strategy. Each week he would send me an email, describing in detail all the things he was going to do. Despite my words of caution, he did launch this campaign and unfortunately it yielded exactly the results that I warned him about. Rather than the several thousand people he expected, a few dozen people signed up, and the folks that did sign up were now committed to only $60 a year. My friend was frustrated with the results and came back to me asking me what to do. Looking at his list of new partners, I realized that several people who were now signed up to give $5 a month could have given $50 or even $500 per month. The lesson learned? Instead of treating people like a variable, inviting them to be part of the five-dollar-a-month club, invite them to truly be partners with you and your organization at a level that makes sense for their unique circumstances.

Do you see the difference between the money-collecting mindset and the relational mindset? Regardless of whether you are utilizing an individual or a group strategy, it is possible to nurture your long-term relationships with people rather than approaching them as a consumer or user. Events and specific campaigns can be a part of this strategy, but they need to be part of a bigger picture.

INDIVIDUAL AND GROUP STRATEGIES

As mentioned in chapter six, there are two ways to raise money—individual and group strategies. When you are talking to someone who is potentially a major donor (a Priority 1 or Priority 2 donor), use the individual strategy; meet with them one-on-one if at all possible. When engaging a Priority 3 donor, you will likely use the group strategy.

Look at your prospect list, sorted by priority, and decide. How should each person be engaged—individually or as part of a group?

For each person, record "group" or "individual" in the solicitation strategy column. You need to make that decision for each person, whether you have three hundred, five hundred, or even two thousand potential donors. Sometimes, when you are dealing with a large list of donors that have previously given, you have to sort your list and use last year's giving to determine who you will pursue individually and who you will purse in a large group. Ideally, look at each person one at a time, because you want to treat people based on their potential to give, not on their current giving.

The individual strategy means meeting with that person face-to-face. If for some reason you can't see them face-to-face, then it's going to take personal emails or handwritten letters, followed by a Zoom or phone call. I've seen some situations where people are raising significant amounts of money but can't spend a lot of time with donors in person. They are fundraising through handwritten letters, Zoom, and phone calls. Although it's not a face-to-face meeting, it's still very personalized.

The group solicitation can take the form of a large group or a small one. You can choose to meet with people through group events, letters, phone calls, and all kinds of other group methodologies.

Make sure to revisit and update your priority prospect list every year, deciding for each donor: At what point and in what context will you be asking them to give? That's taking donors seriously. The most effective way to raise money is to ask everyone face-to-face, based on their financial ability and their interests. But seeing everyone face-to-face is terribly inefficient.

The most efficient way to raise money is to bring everyone into a large group setting, such as a gala, dinner, or auction, and ask everyone to give at the same time. You could also mail fundraising letters to large numbers of donors and prospects. These methods are highly efficient, but not the most effective. In a face-to-face meeting with a Priority 1 donor, it would not be unusual to raise $10,000; rarely does a golf tournament with one hundred people attending raise that amount of money for your organization.

Recently I attended a planning meeting for an organization that had recently been given access to nearly a thousand names of people who might be good prospects for them. What do you do with that? The first idea that surfaced was to send all of those people an email asking them to give. This approach seemed like it would be easy, quick, and cheap.

Often the person who suggests a mass email or letter says something like, "We'll just see what happens." Well, I know what happens. In response to a mass email or letter, the generous people will give small amounts, and the less interested will not give at all. The result will be horrible—like me trying to keep up with professional runners at the start of a marathon.

A better way to respond to this situation is to think through the list of names one by one, creating a plan that maximizes results. The plan will involve dividing the names into different strategies based on how well you know the people on the list.

In the summer of 2019, I got to run in Kenya, in the hardest marathon of my life: the Lewa Safari Marathon. Running 26.2 miles in the Lewa Animal Conservancy was amazing. My finishing time was much, much slower than my best, but I finished the race. I also didn't get eaten by any large animals. (The race organizers literally stationed helicopters overhead and armed rangers along the course to be sure that the Cape buffalo and lions did not get too close to the runners.) I finished the race and had fun—especially because I got to run the first half with my son Max.

The Safari Marathon is a fundraiser for a UK-based charity called Tusk (tusk.org). Tusk raises money not only for animal conservation but also for humanitarian projects in Africa. In exchange for running the race, I was required to raise $5,000. How did I do it? I applied the principle of "Proper Planning Maximizes Results and Minimizes Cost." I could have posted a note on Facebook and asked people to give me money, which is an efficient way to get the word out. But it is not very effective.

Instead, I thought through my list of five-hundred-plus friends on Facebook and sent a personal email to fifteen of those people, asking them individually if they would be willing to support me. Of the fifteen people I asked, sixteen supported me (one person didn't respond, and one person asked two of their friends to join them in supporting me).

By the way, I finished the race in five hours and fifteen minutes and raised over $10,000 for Tusk. The winner, who was from Kenya, finished in three hours and fifteen minutes.

60/40 STRATEGY

Because the individual approach is the most effective, you will use this approach with a smaller percentage of your donors to raise the largest percentage of your goal. You will use the group approach with a larger percentage of your donors to raise the smaller percentage of your goal.

Individual approach: Use with 40 percent of donors / who give 60 percent of your goal.

Group approach: Use with 60 percent of donors / who give 40 percent of your goal.

So what are the percentages? Ideally, the high-level strategy for raising money is fairly simple: 60 percent of your funding should come from 40 percent of your donors. The other 40 percent of your funding comes from the other 60 percent of people.

Now you may be thinking, "Wait, what? Don't you mean the 80/20 rule? The Pareto principle? That 80 percent of your funding comes from 20 percent of your donors?[1] Or maybe the 90/10 rule?"

No, the ideal for your organization really is that 60 percent of your funding comes from 40 percent of your prospects. We're not saying this to be different. We say this because it's vital to have a broad base of support.

In capital campaigns, it is usually true that 10 percent of the people give 90 percent of the gifts. But in the annual fund world, which is what we are focusing on in this book, we want to see a much larger percentage of prospects giving the bulk of the funds. That way, when things change, when donors move, when there's been a change in leadership at an organization, the organization is stable. That stability means that the organization will be able to continue operating and raising the same amount of money.

You don't want to be overly dependent on one or a handful of donors. If you receive a gift that is extremely large relative to your annual fund, use part of it for the annual fund and assign the rest to a special initiative. You might have a donor that gives $50,000 a year and that's way more than you need for the annual fund. So, use $10,000 of that for the annual fund and assign $40,000 for a special project—one that, if the donor were to leave next year, wouldn't cause the organization to have to shut down. Does that mean you have to keep fundraising for the rest of the annual fund? Probably, yes—but remember, a broad base of support means more stability for your organization over time.

When you have a good strategy, you will be both efficient and effective. My friend Tom shared with me what happened when he pursued the "right" people personally rather than just inviting them to an event. Tom works for an amazing organization called St. John's Council on Aging.[2]

Reflecting on his work, he said, "After we talked about how to approach donors relationally based on their connection to our organization, I made a commitment to meet face-to-face with one donor a week and to ask them their story.

"I knew that I shouldn't start by asking them for money, but I should just meet them and get to know them better. So I did. And then, as I met with one of our donors for the first time, he not only told me his story, but he gave me his Mercedes."

"Wait, what?!" I said. "He gave you his Mercedes?"

"Yes," he said, excited. "I got together with the donor, and after I sat and listened to him tell me his story about why he gives to the Council on Aging, he asked me if the Council on Aging would like his Mercedes so it could be sold and the money used to help us serve more seniors in our community."

The moral of the story is not that if you spend time with your donors, they will give you a Mercedes. Rather, there is impressive, amazing power in simply spending time with the right donors. My experience is exactly like the experience that I just related: when we spend time asking our donors their stories and engage people in meaningful conversations, things that we never expected to happen will happen.

For a downloadable PDF summary of key TDS terms and other resources, go to TheFocusGroup.com/partners.

PRACTICE 5
THE ANNUAL PLAN

During the Covid-19 pandemic I got the chance to do something I had always wanted to do—it was a lifelong dream of mine to train for a full Ironman. I had a friend that did this after he retired, and that is what I thought I was going to have to do. But suddenly I found I had the time, with no traveling or flying for work. An Ironman is a 2.4-mile swim, a 112-mile bike ride, followed by a 26.2-mile run. In order to be able to do those distances I had to commit to train for a long time. I started my training in March of 2020 and ran my Ironman in May of 2021. I hired a coach who put together a plan that lasted for fifteen months. Each day I had small steps that led to bigger ones, and on May 22, 2021, I finished the Ironman in a little over fourteen and one-half hours.

Raising money to fund work as a missionary or for an organization is not easy, and is a lot like training for an Ironman. You are reading this book because your fundraising goal is big, but the fundraising task is doable if you follow a plan. After going through the process of preparing a case statement, recruiting leaders to work alongside you, developing a prospects list, and developing a strategy, it's time to create an annual plan, which is identifying all your fundraising efforts and putting them on a calendar.

It's best to raise the funds for your annual budget as early in the new year as possible. In fact, before the new budget year even begins, you should already be engaging major donors. That way, when you enter the new year, you've already raised a large portion of the money. In the first quarter of the budget year you ought to be having group meetings so that by the end of the first quarter you've already raised your annual budget in cash and pledges. So many organizations exhaust themselves in the last month of the budget year, trying to "make budget."

So when you are creating a plan, schedule activities with your major donors, the handful of people who will give most of the money, early in the year so that you gain momentum toward your overall goal. Once you've done your work with your major donors, then it's time to schedule your group events for the year. The plan is simply putting all of those efforts on a timetable so that you can carry out fundraising in a more proactive way.

Remember that the best time to raise money is when we don't need it, and remember that there are key times in the year when fundraising is easier. For example, I have found that getting in touch with donors in the summer to talk about giving can be difficult due to summer vacations. And though many donors make gifts at the end of the calendar year, they are too busy to meet. So I have found that if we raise money early in the year, we get to spend the remaining months—or quarters—engaging donors, thanking them, and inviting them to experience the great work we are doing.

If in the first three months of the year you raise 100 percent of your funding need, you will spend the rest of the year in a very relaxed mode. You are raising money by building trust and drawing donors closer to the heart of your organization and the work you are doing. By the time you enter the fourth quarter of the year, you've already revised the case for the following year, and you're presenting that to major donors. This means you enter the new budget year with a head of steam and can complete your fundraising in the first quarter.

This may sound simple, but it will take a couple of years to get to that point. You cannot make this change all at once. Start by moving your process back one quarter at a time: "Let's raise the funds for our whole budget in the first three quarters." Then, a year or two later: "Let's raise the funds for our whole budget in the first half of the year." Finally, after three or four years, if you've been disciplined in this process, you will be able to raise the funds for your budget in the first quarter. It's very rare, but I know of some organizations that raise their funds before their budget year begins!

CREATING THE PLAN

Now let's walk through what it looks like to create your plan, with the goal of asking once and thanking at least three times.

Our sample plan in table 8.1 shows different categories of fundraising activities that need to take place each year.

Begin with the people who are helping you raise the money needed to achieve your mission: your TDS Team. In the first column, fill in when you plan to have your team meetings. Will you meet every month, every other month, or quarterly?

Table 8.1. Sample plan for fundraising activities

Month	Development Committee / Leadership Team Meetings & Communication	Engaging Priority 1, 2 & 4 Donors	Fundraising Events Priority 3 Donors	Fundraising Materials & Event Prep	Communication (Staff/ Leadership, Donors, Volunteers)
Jul	TDS team meeting	Present case to 1s & 2s and ask for gifts			
Aug				(Retreat); plan for the year	
Sep	TDS team meeting			Revise case statement	
Oct	TDS team meeting			Year-end letter prep and review	
Nov	TDS team meeting			Get case statement approved	
Dec	TDS team meeting	Committee and Tier 1 + 2, Christmas party			

Next, we're going to look at how you're going to thank/ engage your Priority 1, 2, and 4 prospects. Remember, Priority 1 and 2 prospects are the highest capacity givers who are the most involved in your organization. They are also connecting you to their friends, other people of high capacity. Your Priority 4 prospects are people who have maybe given a little bit, or perhaps haven't yet given. However, they have the capacity to be Priority 1 and 2 donors, so you're cultivating them, getting to know them, and engaging them in your organization. So how will you thank/engage this group of people over the course of the year? Fill it in the second column.

Let's say your fiscal year starts in January. If that is the case, then starting in the fall, meet with all of your Priority 1 and 2 prospects to talk to them about their financial giving for the upcoming year. That means setting up meetings with these prospects during September, October, and November and asking them to support your mission financially.

During the rest of the year, thank these people. Call them on the phone, schedule a Zoom meeting with them, go out to coffee or lunch, or send them a handwritten note, just to spend time with them to cultivate the relationship. Schedule these follow-ups into your plan and remember to thank people three times a year and ask just one time. To do this, update your case statement before you meet with them the next year; make sure you update your case in August or September and get your TDS team and board to approve it.

In the next column, we're going to look at fundraising events. Whether it's a banquet in October or a golf tournament in April, fill in all the fundraising events that take place every year. These are the events that are really being targeted at your Priority 3 donors and planned by a separate group of volunteers, and they don't happen without plenty of preparation. But Priority 1 and 2 donors typically still get invited and come (for fellowship, not giving), so we still need to be aware of them.

In the last column, look at your communication with staff, leadership, donors, and volunteers. It's essential to keep people up-to-date consistently. Whether they're giving money or time, how are you going to communicate with them? Don't forget to include everybody who is on your TDS team.

For example, if you send out a quarterly newsletter, write that down in this column. Perhaps you send cards at Christmastime and take gifts to your Priority 1 and 2 donors. Maybe you also send a monthly newsletter or some form of communication to keep your work front of mind. Maybe if something special is

Table 8.2. Sample plan for engaging donors annually

Month	Development Committee / Leadership Team Meetings & Communication	Engaging Priority 1, 2 & 4 Prospects	Fundraising Events Priority 3	Communication (Staff/ Leadership, Donors, Volunteers)
Jan	TDS team meeting	Present case to 1s & 2s and ask for gifts		E-newsletter
Feb	TDS team meeting	Notes to 1s & 2s from someone we serve		E-newsletter
Mar	TDS team meeting	Thank-a-thon on the 30th for 1s & 2s		E-newsletter
Apr	TDS team meeting	Meet with priority 4s to cultivate relationship		E-newsletter
May	TDS team meeting	Notes by committee / staff to priority 1 & 2 monthly donors	Golf tournament	E-newsletter
Jun	TDS team meeting	Success story letter with handwritten note to 1s		E-newsletter
Jul	TDS team meeting	Thank-yous to all		E-newsletter
Aug		Begin priority 1 solicitation		E-newsletter
Sep	TDS team meeting	Finish priority 1 solicitation; start with 2s		E-newsletter
Oct	TDS team meeting	Finish priority 2 solicitation	Fall banquet; handwritten thank-yous to table hosts	E-newsletter
Nov	TDS team meeting	Follow up asks and personal thank-yous to 1s & 2s		E-newsletter
Dec	TDS team meeting	Christmas cards to all, Gifts to 1s		E-newsletter

happening over summer, you send a summer update. Perhaps you have a thank-a-thon to thank people in the late fall. Write in all of your communication tasks.

Once you're finished filling in each column, you will have a yearlong plan that you can share with the people who are helping you on your TDS team. Your team will be prepared for a fantastic year of fundraising!

For a downloadable annual plan and other resources, go to TheFocusGroup.com/partners.

CULTURE

EARNING THE RIGHT TO BE HEARD

I first learned about earning the right to be heard when I was a volunteer Young Life leader. The founder of Young Life came up with this idea to help others understand how to share the gospel with teenagers. Jim Rayburn believed that through building relationships, teenagers would be open to hearing about the truth of God's love for them. The same principle applies to fundraising. Remember that your relationship with each of your donors is just that—a relationship.

We must earn the right to be heard. It's a good idea to get to know someone before asking them for a contribution. We must build real relationships with prospective donors. We've got to actually get to know them, love them, and understand them prior to asking them to be our biggest donor. Developing anything less than a genuine friendship with a prospective donor will earn us the label of "user." Over time we earn the right to ask. In the beginning of a relationship, we can ask people for modest gifts, but so often I have seen younger field staff ask for a very large gift from a donor they barely know. While technically the donor has the money to give, there is not a level of trust that would justify that size of a gift. So we need to start slow and invite people relationally into a deeper partnership over time.

Remember that friendship means listening deeply. Listen for who the person is and what is important to them. Once we've learned who our friend really is, we have earned the right to be heard. It's easy to share our passion for our nonprofit with people who love and care about us. Take advantage of opportunities to introduce newer friends to the work and those the organization serves without asking them for anything. When prospects are good friends who know us and our endeavor, then we can ask for support for our nonprofit.

WHEN DONORS MATTER, CULTURE MATTERS

Remember the principle of fundraising from chapter two: People give to people they know and trust. Before we dive into identifying prospects in chapter seven, I want to focus on the idea of building trust and understanding a donor's culture. Donors can't trust us until we understand who they are! Over the last thirty years in fundraising, I've encountered donors from a wide array of cultural backgrounds. As part of Taking Donors Seriously, I believe we should consider donors individually, approaching each one in a way that makes sense for them. This includes being culturally appropriate, which can take time to learn to do well, especially if we are not aware of the norms of their cultural context.

Many people ask me how to raise money from specific ethnic or cultural groups, but I always steer them away from the underlying assumption that all people of a specific ethnicity or group are the same. Having said that, at The FOCUS Group we are training increasing numbers of executive directors and fundraising staff who are either living overseas or raising money within a specific ethnic community. As a result, over the last several years we have gained insight about fundraising in different cultural contexts.

As part of our team at The FOCUS Group, one of our consultants, Justin Forbes, has been a key player in training people from diverse backgrounds who are successfully raising money in various cultural contexts. He shared an excellent example of how cultural context could affect fundraising:

> A recent client of mine is a young up-and-coming leader in a major campus ministry. He is Chinese American and so are many of his donors. During our training together, we spent many hours navigating the terrain of culture as a means of communicating well with older, more traditional Chinese American donors, and younger, more culturally fluid Chinese American donors. It was fascinating to explore this reality as together we remained doggedly committed to loving and serving these individual donors, honoring and respecting their sense of what would be appropriate.

The young campus minister still needed to raise support, so his goal was to discern not *if* to ask, but *how*: how he would lovingly, wisely, with the donor in mind, ask for their sacrificial gift. He explained that in his culture it could be considered disrespectful for someone to make a direct ask of a donor and that an indirect approach would be more honoring to the donor.

So he brainstormed all the ways to make an ask that was clear and articulate, yet indirect. The giving plan and budget was still part of the case statement, and of course he asked permission to have a discussion about the organization and its funding needs. But he framed the conversation around a deferred decision left to the donor—a more indirect approach.

This doesn't mean that this was the approach for all his Chinese American donors. A lot of thought was put into what would be most culturally sensitive or appropriate for everyone. His approach was different with younger Chinese American donors who weren't as concerned with some of the cultural protocol. His approach was different still when he approached White donors or African American donors. What is important is to pursue the most faithful approach to asking each donor.

Embracing the Taking Donors Seriously approach means considering how culture, race, gender, age, and other factors might affect one's ability to hear the vision that is expressed in a case statement. If we are going to be truly donor-centered, then we must remain open to all the ways in which God has been present, has moved, and is moving in different cultures.

You might start by asking yourself these questions:

1. Is there a person who understands the unique cultural context that I can practice my pitch with and get honest feedback from?

2. Who has gone before me and worked in this space that could help me gain an understanding of cultural differences?

3. Does my approach take seriously the culture of this donor?

I strongly encourage all of us to be engaged in becoming aware of our own cultural biases; we all have them and they influence us all the time. Spend time beginning to grow generally in this area, and then the overall growth you encounter will influence your ability to be a great crosscultural fundraiser. I also highly recommend the group Bible study experience offered by the amazing ministry Arrabon, entitled "A People, a Place, and a Just Society."[1] I would also recommend a book by Austin Channing Brown, *I'm Still Here*. While neither the study nor the book deals directly with fundraising, they will help you better understand who you are and how your experience and the people you are engaging with may have a different cultural experience than you.

THE ASK
GETTING STARTED

Congratulations! You've made it. At this point, you've learned about the six principles and five practices of Taking Donors Seriously. You've learned about developing a *case statement*, identifying your potential *leadership* team, and clarifying who your best donor *prospects* are, as well as how to create an effective and efficient *strategy* to ask and thank, all written down in your *annual plan*. Now it's time to put it all together and execute it. We have arrived at the stage when we ask donors to become partners with us in our work!

Friends, I have good news for you—it's a lot easier than you think. First, you need to ask an important question: Where are you in your fundraising year? If it's the start of a brand-new year for your organization, then it's straightforward to take the plan you put together and implement it. But if you're halfway through the year and you've met with some of your donors and not others, then you need to take a step back and evaluate how you can begin to implement TDS from your current vantage point.

Whether you are an individual staff worker with a goal of $50,000, or an organization with a goal of $500,000, the best way to get started is to evaluate your received and pledged gifts for the current year. This will indicate how much additional money you need to raise.

Once you have established how much (additional) money you need to raise, set an initial target goal. Then, determine the smallest number of donors you need to ask to accomplish that goal by your target date. Ultimately you should start with your Priority 1 donors.

Whether you are in the middle of your year or about to start a new one, make sure you adjust your plan to this starting point.

ASKING FOR MONEY: THE GROUND RULES

As we begin to discuss the asking process, I need to start with two very important ground rules when it comes to asking for money.

1. Always let the person know ahead of time when you are planning to ask.

2. Ask people for something they can give.

We have found that one of the biggest criticisms of fundraisers is that they surprise people by asking for money when a potential donor isn't expecting it. This doesn't build healthy relationships over time, and then people will avoid fundraisers when they see them, thinking they might use the opportunity to ask for money. Let's be very respectful of people by letting them know ahead of time that we're planning to ask.

Secondly, we respect people by asking them for something they can give. There's a terrible philosophy among some fundraisers: if you ask someone for twice what you want them to give, then you're more likely to get what you want. This approach does not honor the relationships. In fact, this practice threatens relationships. So, we ask them for something that they can give. I have heard concerns about "under-asking," but it is not a problem if we are committed to being in a partnership with our donors. It is okay to leave money on the table if we are committed to being in a partnership with a donor over a lifetime.

When I was in charge of fundraising for the mission of Young Life, my boss, the president of Young Life, asked me to meet with one of his best friends and ask for a large gift. I scheduled a time to meet with "John" and told him that his best friend Denny Rydberg had asked me to meet with him, that I wanted to get together with him to talk about his annual gift to Young Life. John was very open to meeting and we met for breakfast on a brisk winter morning in Orlando.

We had breakfast and at the end of the time I shared with him our case statement, showed him the budget, answered some questions, and then asked him for a gift using the gift chart. I asked John for a gift with a low and a high that was based on what my boss told me to ask for. John instantly looked offended, so I did what I often recommend—run and hide. No, seriously—I responded verbally to the nonverbal message he sent and said, "You seem taken aback by what I just asked you for." John responded by saying, "I am a little offended by the huge sum of money you just asked me for. What right do you have to ask for such a large gift? We just met."

I replied, "I don't have a right to ask you for such a large gift, but my boss, Denny, asked me to ask you for that gift based on your relationship with him."

John then responded by saying "Okay, that makes sense. I can give that gift."

Having said that, when you ask to meet with someone, if your plan is to just get to know them or share your case with them and not ask them for money, tell them that too. Let the person know that you're not going to ask! Honor the relationship by letting the donor know what to expect. That way, you are building the relationship for the long term, not around fundraising but around the actual cause of the organization. Remember, you are building a genuine relationship with them. Don't ask them for money without first letting them know that the question is coming.

NO WINE BEFORE ITS TIME

Orson Welles, the American writer and director most famous for his film *Citizen Kane*, starred in a famous commercial in 1978. The distinguished Welles promoted Paul Masson wine with a memorable slogan: "We will sell no wine before its time."

Fundraising and wine have a lot in common. It's true that serving wine at a charity auction may increase reckless giving, but this is not what I am suggesting (nor do I think it's an ethical thing to do!). Rather, I want to highlight that there is a right time to talk to a donor about making a gift, just as there is a right time to sell wine: when the barreled wine has been sufficiently aged for bottling.

I often meet with clients who embark on the fundraising journey with enthusiasm, and after hearing about a new prospective donor they want to begin by asking the donor to make a gift—often at their first meeting! While this strategy seems very efficient, it is not very effective. In my experience, it's necessary to meet with a donor several times—a series of meetings that allow the relationship to develop—before asking for a gift.

I can't overstate the importance of this process. Several years ago, I met with a major donor who was a significant giver to one of my clients. I was meeting with them to talk about a potential gift to my client, and before we could begin, they poured out their frustrations about another nonprofit. The president of the first organization had come to meet with them, they said, and before even getting to know what they were passionate about, he asked them for a large gift. It felt transactional, they said, and uncomfortable. As a result, they made a modest gift—by their own admission not nearly the gift that they actually wanted to make! My client, however, did not share this hasty approach, and the couple went on to make a significant gift to them.

As we explore the fundraising process, I challenge you to go slowly. Anything good takes time. Make sure you have multiple meetings prior to an ask. Sit down, get to know the donor, and remember, "We will sell no wine before its time."

THE ASKING PROCESS

Practically, the asking process has four stages. The first three stages are about cultivating the relationship and include an ask that has nothing to do with money. Only the final stage involves an ask for money. Starting with a bird's eye view, the four stages are as follows:

1. The Informal Conversation

2. The Tour

3. The Presentation of the Case

4. The Ask

Within each stage, there are four steps: invitation, preparation, meeting, and follow-up. The entire asking process might look something like this:

1. The Informal Conversation
   - Invitation
   - Preparation
   - The meeting
   - Follow-up

2. The Tour
   - Invitation
   - Preparation
   - The meeting
   - Follow-up

3. The Presentation of the Case
   - Invitation
   - Preparation
   - The meeting
   - Follow-up

4. The Ask
   - Invitation
   - Preparation
   - The meeting
   - Follow-up

Now, this is not to say that you must have four separate meetings with every major donor before making an ask. However, if someone you know has never heard of your organization, and they fit the profile of a potential Priority 1 donor, then you will probably have four distinct meetings with them before you get to ask them for a gift. Cultivating that relationship over time is more important than getting to the ask. But though there are four steps, we must also be aware of the donor's prompts. A retired donor in Florida may have more time to engage than a busy New York City donor who wants to meet only once. Our commitment is to engaging donors in genuine relationship, but we can't force a donor to follow our plan if they are wanting to move quicker or slower.

STAGE 1: THE INFORMAL CONVERSATION

The informal conversation means you are simply getting together with a potential donor on the phone, Zoom, or for lunch or coffee where you casually introduce your organization to them. You should intentionally "take money off the table" before getting together with them. Spend time getting to know them and share why you are so excited about your cause or organization. If you already are friends with this person, then this meeting has a different feel than if you are meeting the person for the first time. Ultimately this meeting is to explore whether this prospect would be a good donor for your organization. If during the informal conversation you discover something about them that makes you sure they would not be a good fit, but possibly would be for a different organization, be open to that. Ultimately this is a discovery meeting.

During each stage, ask a question that leads to deeper engagement—and hopefully to the next stage. During the informal conversation stage, you might ask, "Would you like to take a tour and see for yourself?"

Sometimes, though, the process is much slower. The informal conversation may simply lead to another informal conversation. For example, you may go to meet with a prospect for coffee. Before ever mentioning your organization, they tell you that their daughter is getting married. The prospect is brimming over with excitement, so you spend the rest of the time talking about that wedding. In this case, your next meeting would be another initial meeting, not the tour. This is not a detour. You are building a relationship with people over time. Having said this, you can't not talk to the donor about your organization forever—the reason you asked for the initial meeting was to share with them about your organization.

STAGE 2: THE TOUR

In your follow-up from the informal conversation, invite them to take a tour. Invite them to come and see—come and meet a graduate, come explore the facility, come serve soup—just come see what you're doing together. The tour is a powerful moment because the potential donor will get to see the organization in action. You're inviting them to be a part of it.

Tours can take many different forms. You can invite someone to literally come and walk around the place where you do your work, or you can bring a tour to a prospect by inviting a person your organization has reached to come on an appointment with you. One of the blessings that has come from the pandemic is that most people are very comfortable with Zoom, so you can now have a Zoom meeting with a donor and take them on a tour of your work. A Zoom tour is especially helpful if your donor is in another town!

I remember a few years ago when one of the staff workers I was working with from InterVarsity had an inductive Bible study with some of his donors. The Bible study itself was a great thing to do with donors, but he was also taking them on a tour, because the Bible study he led with them was the same one that he had led with a group of college students the week before.

After the tour, the natural progression is to ask if you can sit down and share the case statement, which will further explain the vision of your organization.

STAGE 3: THE PRESENTATION OF THE CASE

Following the tour, the next stage involves sitting down with the potential donor to present the case and show them the details of your organization. Presenting the case is something that is best done in person, but can also be done on Zoom or even over the phone. When sitting down with a donor, start by showing them the theme of the case statement and explaining why you chose that theme and how it relates to your work. Following this, do not walk them through every page (unless they are brand new to your organization), but rather pick a few of the ten elements of the case statement that you think would be especially interesting to them. But always include the budget and the gift plan—don't shy away from the numbers. Do make sure that when you invite them to this stage, you reassure them that today is not about asking them for a gift but sharing more details about your organization with them. Specifically, after you show them the budget for your organization, it is important to pause and ask them if they have any questions. This pause after presenting the budget is important, because if they have questions about the budget, they will likely not be ready to look at or consider being one of the donors represented on the gift plan.

At the end of this meeting, ask them if you can follow up with them in a few days or weeks to set up a time to talk about making a gift. This question sets you up for the final stage—the ask.

STAGE 4: THE ASK

The ask meeting is extremely important—but sometimes it is not an actual fourth meeting. Following the case meeting you may have the fourth meeting in person, but it can also be a follow-up phone call or Zoom meeting. But, be sure to remind the donor ahead of time that you would like to talk to them about a gift. Remember rule number one: Always let people know when you are going to talk to them about making a gift.

At the ask meeting, refer to the gift plan page in your case statement—even if your meeting is on the phone; you will have left the case statement with them after you presented it in your previous meeting. In most cases, talk to prospects about a range rather than a specific number. Conveniently, this range is the low and high that you have pre-calculated when you completed your segmented prospect list. Of course the low and high that you have for them may not be printed exactly as such in your case statement, so use the general low and high numbers that are close to what you have projected for them.

THE FOUR STEPS OF EACH STAGE

During each stage of the process, there is a four-step pattern to follow. Follow these steps whether you are having an initial meeting, hosting a tour, giving a presentation of the case, or finally making the ask.

Step 1: Invitation. The invitation is the most important step. When inviting someone to meet, make sure that the closest person—the one most important to them—is asking them to meet. Ideally, that person also needs to be at the actual meeting. When you are inviting someone to meet, be upfront and clear about the reason for the meeting. Simply ask the person if they would be willing to get together with you to talk about your work. Ask them about a specific time and place to meet. Your invitation to meet can be done by text, over the phone, or via email. Communicate with your prospect in the way you normally communicate with them.

Step 2: Preparation. After you get the meeting scheduled, you need to prepare for the meeting. Prior to the meeting, do research on the prospect's past involvement with your organization and your knowledge of them. If you're going into a meeting with someone who cares about your mission and can give a lot of money, don't wing it. Reacquaint yourself with the people you are meeting, their history of support or involvement with your organization, and any items or factors that might influence their decision.

For example, if you are meeting with a couple in their late forties or early fifties and they have three kids in college, you ought to temper your expectations because they probably have some pretty significant tuition bills. If you're meeting with a young professional just starting a dental practice or some other business, that might factor into your expectations as well—that person is going to be putting a lot of money into starting their business. On the other hand, if people are in their late fifties or sixties and just sold a business, they could be in a position to give a very large gift. Pay attention to the seasons of people's lives so that you can be prepared and set your expectations appropriately.

I was once solicited by a nonprofit that I helped start twenty-five years ago. The person asking me for the gift had no idea about my past involvement (and love) for the organization and missed an opportunity to engage me in a much more meaningful way. If they had done more research, they would have asked me to tell my story, which would have reconnected me to their organization and I would have given a much larger gift.

Step 3: The meeting. Now let's look at the actual meeting. Whenever you meet with a donor, these four elements should be present:

- Clarifying how much time they have for the meeting
- Engaging in casual conversation
- Having a conversation about your organization
- Asking a question that leads to further engagement

When meeting with a donor, particularly if you are meeting over a meal, you should start by clarifying how much time they have to meet. You may be assuming they have an hour, when in fact they have thirty minutes. Once you clarify the amount of time they have for the meeting take about half of that time just talking and connecting. Engage the donor in conversation about what matters to them—their family, their business, their extracurricular activities, their interests, other nonprofits they support, a whole range of things! If you have prepared properly, you have reminded yourself of what matters to this donor and then intentionally asked them about it.

I remember once meeting with a major donor and forgetting to ask them about the recent marriage of their only daughter. They brought it up during our meeting, but I left that meeting feeling like I would have done a better job if I had reviewed my notes from the previous meeting and led with a question about something that obviously meant a great deal to the donor.

During that first half of the meeting, don't try to navigate toward talking about your organization or mission. Encourage them to talk about themselves. The person may even say, "Well, you didn't come to hear me talk about myself," and encourage you to talk about your organization. Respond respectfully, but then turn the conversation back toward the person and continue listening. This extended period of listening will help you build a genuine friendship.

Hopefully, people will feel comfortable because you have listened to them and genuinely cared about them—but if they don't want to talk about themselves and would rather ask you questions about you and your family, then allow the donor to lead. The point is to be natural and engage with them relationally.

By the way, if you have the case statement with you at this meeting (this is for when you reach the third stage of presenting the case statement or for when you make the ask), don't bring it out and put it on the table just yet. Instead, hang on to it until you have spent that first half of the meeting engaging with the donor. Often, they will say something important for you to know before you transition to talking about your organization. Sometimes there's even a direct connection between what's going on in their lives and what you want to share.

The second part of the meeting is telling your story in a way that fits the donor. When presenting your case statement, remember that you can approach it horizontally or vertically. A horizontal approach means speaking very broadly about your organization, thumbing through the case, and just referring to the headlines. You won't give many details unless asked. If you're sharing the case with someone who has some expertise and may want to ask specific questions, use a more vertical approach. You might say, "I know you're interested in how we are reaching this particular segment of the population, so here are some of the strategies we are using." In this situation, it is appropriate to give quite a bit of detail, because this is interesting and engaging to the donor.

While you are preparing for the meeting, decide in advance how you will approach the case statement. If you are going to go into more depth (the vertical approach), you may need to bring some additional materials that would convey those details.

The fourth part of the meeting is asking a question. Whenever you ask someone to meet with you and talk about your organization, you should always end with a question that leads to deeper engagement. The question doesn't always have to be about money, but each step has a question that goes a little like this:

- Question for the casual conversation step: Would you be willing to come and take a tour of our organization?

- Question for the tour step: Is there a time I can sit down with you to share with you the details of our organization?

- Question for the case step: Can I follow up with you in a couple of weeks and meet with you about making a gift?

- Question for the ask step: Would you consider a gift in this range?

Step 4: Follow-up. Once you meet with a donor, then we reach the stage that seems to be most challenging for organizations—the follow-up. I have probably said this about a thousand times, but the number-one failure in fundraising is a lack of follow-up.

If the donor makes a commitment to give to your organization at the meeting, obviously you will want to thank them in the moment and say whatever is appropriate for the context. But then it's crucial to follow up with a thank-you using the same method of communication that you normally use to communicate with them (email, handwritten note, text, etc.). This

follow-up communication should include their commitment—
not just the amount of money, but also the time frame of the
gift. If they did not include the time frame for when they will
be giving the gift, it is okay to use this opportunity to clarify
that. My experience is that most of the time you will not need
to send a pledge card for them to fill out, but sometimes that
can be helpful.

Maybe you've been one of those fundraisers, so excited to
return from a meeting with a donor, saying, "You know how
we thought they'd give $5,000? Well, they gave $10,000! We're
so happy that we can't believe it! They're going to give $10,000!"
And then someone responded, saying, "That's great! When are
they going to give it?" And suddenly, your mind went blank;
there was no mention of a time frame.

Timing is important. When you discuss a gift and someone
says, "I'd like to seriously consider that," you could say,
"That's wonderful! Would you consider giving half of that
before the end of the calendar year, and the other half at the
end of our fiscal year?"

In a way, referencing the amount and the time frame for the
gift is simply clarifying that you really heard what you thought
you heard. If for some reason that wasn't clear, you can say in
the follow-up communication, "Please get back to me if I've
misstated." In this situation, it is fine to invite someone to make
a correction in terms of their commitment.

Following up with donors is critical. We must always remember to keep the ball in our court. Don't end the meeting
and say, "When you decide what to give, let me know." Instead,
say something like, "Is it okay if I follow up with you in a week
to talk about the pledge or gift you may want to give?"

If you don't get a commitment during the meeting itself, make sure to engage them soon after—definitely within a couple of weeks, if not within a week. Reconnect with them and see what they're thinking in terms of their commitment; it's important to close that loop. If you do get a commitment over the phone, then thank them appropriately. And make sure to write that follow-up note!

If the meeting is for cultivation only, rather than an ask, then engage them again about a time when you can talk to them about a gift. After the cultivation occurs, you can engage them to make a commitment. Make sure to follow up on that meeting, too. Are you getting the picture? Following up on every meeting is essential.

It's easy to be overwhelmed at this point, so be sure to tackle this process in the smaller steps I've described. You're doing great. Don't try to do everything at once. Remember the vital principle of Taking Donors Seriously: Proper planning maximizes results and minimizes costs.

THREE WAYS TO ASK FOR A GIFT

My experience is that that most people will do a good job on each of the steps and stages of the asking process, but get very nervous when it comes to the actual financial ask. Let's think back to our fundraising rules—both rules will help us with that nervousness. First, remember that the number one rule in fundraising is that you always let someone know ahead of time when you are going to be asking them for a gift. When you give them a heads-up, you are taking care of the relationship you have with them. Rule number two? You always want to ask someone for an amount they can say yes to. Again, you are operating in a way that is straightforward, honoring the relationship.

When it comes down to making that ask, there are three ways to ask for money, because there is no one-size-fits-all for how to ask someone to make a gift. Here are the three ways to ask for a gift:

- Ask for a specific amount. (You should do this only about 10 percent of the time.)

- Ask for a range between two numbers. (Ask in this way about 80 percent of the time.)

- Show them the budget and leave it wide open for the person to decide. (About 10 percent of the time.)

1. Asking for a specific amount. When you don't know someone very well, ask them for a specific amount that you know they can say yes to. This person may already be connected to your organization, but they just haven't drawn very close at this point. When you're asking someone like this for money, I suggest aiming low; don't ask them for too much. Instead, from the three different levels shown in the gift plan, you might point to the lowest level and say, "Would you consider giving $250 now and again before the end of the year?" Keep the ask nominal, even if they have the capacity to give a big gift. At this point, you want to focus on the relationship—not the money. Don't try to go right to the top tier of the gift plan. That's not a good way to build a relationship with them. Instead, ask for something that you know they can say yes to. The best part is that now you get to thank them for their gift!

Several years ago, a friend of mine got the chance to have dinner with a football player Tim Tebow. She was thrilled with the opportunity, and called me to ask if she should ask him to fund the rest of her budget. After all, he was famous for his generosity. Her budget was modest—she only needed around $25,000 to make budget. I cautioned against her asking for this sized gift, knowing that if she asked him for a gift of that size, he would probably refer her to his foundation—which would likely lead to a long process with an unclear future. I suggested that she instead ask him for a modest gift to provide a scholarship for one of her students for an upcoming retreat. My friend was frustrated with my suggestion but reluctantly asked for the gift that was a hundred times smaller—$250. The famous football player said yes on the spot. As a result, my friend was able to follow up with him and share the impact that the small gift had had on one of her students. There were two results: a changed life for the scholarship student, and an opportunity for an ongoing relationship with this celebrity. (My friend ended up leaving ministry for personal reasons, not due to funding. So unfortunately, this story does not end with the athlete or his foundation giving a larger gift, because he was never given the chance!)

So, with new prospects, asking with a range is problematic because they don't know what we need. Instead, ask for a specific amount that they can easily say yes to so that you can continue developing your relationship with them.

Go slow, resist the temptation to dishonor the relationship, and remember that it is okay to "leave money on the table" because you are not leaving the table. It's better to develop the relationship over the long term. Rather than submit a proposal to a foundation that probably would have gone nowhere, by asking for a smaller gift, my friend was able to develop a new relationship between her organization and this football player.

2. Asking for a range. The second way to ask for a gift is to describe a range by pointing to one of the gift plan sections. This is why we encourage you to divide the gift plan into three distinct sections—so you can use it to ask for a range! You can point to the middle section and say, "You know, you've been so generous to our organization. We've appreciated that so much. Would you consider making a gift at this level?" It will be clear that you are not asking for a specific amount but asking for an amount in a particular range.

Asking with a range is by far the least threatening way to ask for a gift, but unfortunately most people rarely use this approach. You should be asking for a gift in this way *most* of the time. We suggest that you ask for a range that reflects the low and high that you and your TDS team have predetermined that the person can give. Also, remember to talk about the timing. Do you want them to give monthly, quarterly, or annually?

3. Leaving it wide open. When you know someone extremely well, and they have previously or repeatedly blown you away with their generosity, your goal is to "get out of the way" of the giver. In this situation, leave it wide open for them to decide. In some sense, suggesting a specific amount or even a range to these very special people is ignoring their previous generosity. For these particular people, show them the gift plan and say instead, "This is our strategy. We've given a lot of attention to figuring out how to raise our budget. In light of your generosity and your love of our organization, where do you see yourself? We'd like to open it up to you." When you take this approach, you are honoring the donor and getting out of the way of the giver.

Another common mistake is to ask our closest friends, who have been generous with us in the past, for a specific amount that is much lower than they would have given. You already know that they love you. Show them the gift plan and leave it wide open.

One day at a training event, I met a woman who had a reputation for being very wealthy and very generous. She was on the board of a particular college, and she told me a story about the college coming to her and asking her for $100,000. She asked me, "Why did they ask me for that amount? I don't understand. I had in my mind that I was going to give them $600,000." She remarked, "I felt very uncomfortable. I didn't like being approached that way. I wanted to give them a large gift." When people have been generous, especially people with a lot of capacity, get out of their way! Invite them to give and trust them to continue to be generous to your organization.

Regardless of which of these three approaches you are using, always show the gift plan from the case statement. Remember, people give when they are asked and shown how. The gift plan is how they are "shown how." Unfortunately, most of the time people don't use the case statement, rarely use a range, and tend to leave the amount wide open. At the end of the meeting you should offer and be prepared to pay; but my experience is that 99 percent of the time the donor will pay. If you have a gift to leave with them, please be sure it is meaningful to them and not just a trinket with your organization's logo on it. I have so many mugs, pens, and journals with random organizations on them—but I can think back a few years to when an executive director, who as asking us for money, brought my wife dark

chocolate from Switzerland, which was very meaningful because they had remembered that my wife loves dark chocolate.

WHAT TO DO WHEN A DONOR SAYS NO

Early in the book I shared six principles of fundraising—the
sixth principle is that a no has a context. Along the way, when
we ask a donor for anything and their response is "No," we must
stay engaged and try to understand why they have said no. If
we have practiced the permission-based fundraising approach—
walking the donor through multiple steps prior to an ask,
keeping money "off the table" along the way—and then ask the
donor to meet with us to talk about making a gift and they say
"No," there is a good reason why they haven't said "Yes." In my
experience there are three reasons:

1. They still have questions that have not been answered.

2. We have asked them for the wrong amount or the wrong
   part of our work.

3. The timing of when they can give is off.

With these three reasons in mind, if you are in a meeting with
a donor and they do not say why their answer is no, your job is
to attempt to clarify which of the three are at play. You can ask
a simple follow-up question to clarify the context of the no.

Here are some example questions you can memorize:

"Thank you so much for meeting with me today and allowing me to talk to you about a gift. Can you say more
about why you can't commit to helping? Do you have any
unanswered questions?"

"Did I ask you to support a part of our work that resonates
with you?"

"Is there a better time of the year for me to talk with you about making a gift?"

ONGOING DONOR ENGAGEMENT

After you have taken a donor through the four steps of the asking process, you simply start over with step one—the casual conversation. Think of this as the yearlong plan for engaging your donors over a lifetime. At this point the donor is a friend and partner, so your engagement is more a casual reconnection time than a meeting to explore their interest in your organization. Your year two tour is different, maybe focusing on an aspect of your work that you have now learned is more interesting to them. Since you previously presented a case to them, they will just be looking at the things that have been updated—a new story about a life that was changed or some of your accomplishments (and of course your budget). Finally, the ask for support will also be somewhat easier, as they will know better what to expect.

Occasionally, for lots of reasons, a person will stop supporting you. Maybe they lost their job, or maybe a personal situation caused them to need to redirect their giving away from your work. I encourage you to remember the fifth principle we have been talking about in this chapter: A no is never forever. My advice is to treat people like they have the potential to give, not how they are giving in the moment. And if they have been a huge investor in your work in the past and they can't give anymore, or maybe never again, keep informing and communicating with them based on their historical giving to you.

A few years ago, when I was still raising support, a donor who had been supporting my work for ten years had to stop giving.

If I added up how much they had given over the previous ten years, it would have equaled a whole year of my support. When they shared with me that they could not continue giving, I told them that they were permanently a part of my support team and that I would continue to inform them and update them about our work for the rest of their life—which I did. I maintained the relationship for an additional five years. When they passed away two things happened: their son asked me to speak at the funeral because of the close relationship the donor and I had, and upon my own research, I found that this donor, even though they had not given in the last five years, was still one of the top five donors who had historically supported my work.

For some practical examples and videos on the asking process please go to TheFocusGroup.com/partners.

BEING FULLY FUNDED
SAYING YES

Some years ago a close friend of mine, Ronnie, made a leap of faith. He decided to leave his position in law enforcement and go on staff with Evangelism Explosion (EE) to help people learn how to share their faith. Going into full-time ministry where you have to raise your own support can be daunting; but for Ronnie, career transition was even harder because he was in his early sixties. He worked to raise the money for a while and then got stuck, so he asked me for help. Ronnie ended up being the very first person to complete our online training for Taking Donors Seriously. After completing the training, Ronnie raised all of his support and my wife and I had the chance to become donors. For the next ten years, Ronnie and his wife, Lynn, trained thousands of people to share their faith. The true impact of their work will never be known this side of heaven.

Several years after starting to support Ronnie, I get a letter in the mail from the president of Evangelism Explosion. He was reaching out to all their major donors, asking them to pray for the funding of their ministry, because things had gotten hard recently. Apparently, my wife and I had supported Ronnie for long enough at a low level that the total of all these gifts qualified us as major donors.

Upon receiving the letter, I did pray, but I also called up the president of EE and offered to have The FOCUS Group help them with fundraising. Together we helped EE launch and complete a $19 million campaign that allowed them to move beyond surviving to thriving. Through this campaign, they exponentially grew their work of equipping people around the world to share their faith.

Ronnie recently passed away after a battle with cancer. Before saying goodbye, I got to spend some time with him, and I could not help but think about the huge impact Ronnie had had. Just by saying yes, he became part of something much larger than himself. As his peers headed out to play golf, he went into full-time ministry, and as a direct result, Evangelism Explosion connected to The FOCUS Group and launched a campaign to enhance and grow their work. Ronnie had no idea. He simply said yes to what was in front of him.

Our lives exist within a larger framework of what God is doing. We only get to see that story unfolding every so often, but we can step forward and say yes to what we are called to do. We can have faith that God will do immeasurably more than we ask or imagine. Sometimes we catch a glimpse of it, as I did with Ronnie's story, and sometimes we don't, but I challenge you to say yes in your fundraising work.

I wrote this book to give you a practical framework to use to fully fund your work based on biblical principles. Remember, fundraising is all about relationships. The more fundraising reflects a relational approach, the more you're going to enjoy it and the more your donors will become partners with you in advancing the kingdom of God.

ACKNOWLEDGMENTS

Over the years I have been mentored by so many people that I could not begin to name them all, but I am grateful for my family—my wife, my four children, and my parents.

In addition, over the years there have been different people that God has put into my life to help me learn more about him and fundraising. I think of these people often and am grateful for the role they have played in my development.

In North Palm Beach—Jim Chesnes, Steve and Fran Godfrey, and Steve Godfrey Jr.

In Gainesville—Antley Fowler and Robert Morris

In St. Augustine—Martha Shinn and Wayne Byerly

In Orlando—Charlie Scott, Rick Dillard, and Curtis McWilliams

While working for Young Life nationally—Greg Kinberg, Denny Rydberg, and John Wagner

Since leaving Young Life staff—Bill Hautt, Ted Rodgers, and Scott Rodin

Lastly I want to thank Tom Lin, Al Hsu, Kate Permuy, Shannon Marion, and Hannah Kaminer for their help with creating this book!

NOTES

1. DOING IT DIFFERENTLY

[1]"Giving USA 2021: In a Year of Unprecedented Events and Challenges, Charitable Giving Reached a Record $471.44 Billion in 2020," Philanthropy Network, June 15, 2021, https://philanthropynetwork.org/news/giving-usa -2021-year-unprecedented-events-and-challenges-charitable-giving-reached-record -47144.

2. SIX KEY PRINCIPLES OF FUNDRAISING

[1]Joshua Morrison, "Testimonial" (video), The FOCUS Group, accessed April 22, 2022, https://thefocusgroup.com/testimonials/.

[2]Jorg Wenig, "Teenager Mekonnen's Stunning Marathon Debut Win in Dubai," World Athletics, January 24, 2014, https://worldathletics.org/news/report /standard-chartered-dubai-marathon-tsegaye-mek.

[3]Conor O'Clery, *The Billionaire Who Wasn't: How Chuck Feeney Made and Gave Away a Fortune Without Anyone Knowing* (New York: Public Affairs, 2007).

[4]Jim Dwyer, "'James Bond of Philanthropy' Gives Away the Last of His Fortune," *New York Times*, January 5, 2017, www.nytimes.com/2017/01/05/nyregion/james -bond-of-philanthropy-gives-away-the-last-of-his-fortune.html.

4. PRACTICE 1: THE CASE STATEMENT

[1]Good News Church (website), accessed April 26, 2022, www.goodnewsloves.com.

[2]Kent M. Keith, "The Paradoxical Commandments," Anyway: The Paradoxical Commandments (website), accessed April 26, 2022, www.paradoxical commandments.com.

[3]"How Much Did the Apollo Program Cost?" The Planetary Society, accessed April 26, 2022, www.planetary.org/space-policy/cost-of-apollo.

[4]Billy Graham Evangelistic Association, "Billy Graham: Pastor to Presidents," May 17, 2021, https://billygraham.org/gallery/billy-graham-pastor-to-the -presidents/.

5. PRACTICE 2: LEADERSHIP

[1]Jim Rayburn, *From Bondage to Liberty: Dance, Children, Dance* (Colorado Springs: Morningstar Press, 2000), 36.

[2]Chase Peterson-Withorn, "Forbes' 36th Annual World's Billionaires List: Facts and Figures 2022," *Forbes*, April 5, 2022, www.forbes.com/sites/chasewithorn /2022/04/05/forbes-36th-annual-worlds-billionaires-list-facts-and-figures -2022/?sh=3c63ed77e303.

7. PRACTICE 4: THE STRATEGY

[1]"Pareto Principle," Investopedia, April 7, 2022, www.investopedia.com/terms/p /paretoprinciple.asp.

[2]St. John's County Council on Aging, accessed April 26, 2022, www.coasjc.org.

9. CULTURE

[1]"A People, A Place, and a Just Society" (course), Arrabon, accessed April 26, 2022, https://arrabon.com/a-people-a-place-and-a-just-society/.

ABOUT THE AUTHOR

Brad Layland, CFRE, received his BA in communications from the University of Florida and his MA in theology from Fuller Theological Seminary. He and his wife, Wendy, reside in St. Augustine, Florida, and have four children. Brad enjoys running marathons, skiing, investing in real estate, entrepreneurship, and traveling with his family. Over the past twenty years, he has completed over fifty marathons and two Ironman Triathlons.

Brad is the CEO of The FOCUS Group. He joined the firm in 2012 after a twenty-year career with Young Life where he was the Chief Development Officer. Since purchasing The FOCUS Group in 2015, the firm has grown to be ten times larger, serving over one hundred Christian ministries through a team of thirty staff and consultants. Brad's expertise includes providing high level fundraising counsel and training to nonprofit organizations. In recent years he has led capital campaigns for Inter-Varsity Christian Fellowship ($81 million), Union Rescue Mission ($83 million), The Bowery Mission ($27 million), and Veritas School ($5.3 million).

Brad is also the founder of Endless Summer Realty, the largest residential real estate brokerage in St. Augustine, closing over $250 million in transactions in 2021. He is a founding board member of Veritas Classical School, which has grown to over two hundred students in five years, and launched an annual "Giving Day" in St. Augustine that has become a platform for local nonprofits to raise hundreds of thousands of dollars and establish relationships with new donors. His entrepreneurial success has allowed Brad to personally experience the joy of generosity and gain a special understanding of the mindset of a major donor.

For more information about Brad Layland visit his website or social media pages:

https://bradlayland.com (where you can also subscribe to his blog)

www.linkedin.com/in/bradlayland

www.facebook.com/brad.layland

To subscribe to Brad's podcast please go to

https://podcasts.apple.com/us/podcast/the-taking-donors-seriously-podcast/id769463284

For more information about The FOCUS Group go to

https://thefocusgroup.com

Your Vision, Fully Funded.

For over 40 years, **The FOCUS Group** has served nonprofits by providing strategic fundraising counsel to help them reach and exceed their fundraising goals. Our mission is to advance the kingdom of God by building trusting relationships with our clients and providing the expertise and guidance to accelerate the funding of their vision.

Our counsel is based on trusted, time-tested, and effective strategies to help you:

- Cultivate relationships of generosity with major donors
- Design a sustainable approach to fundraising
- Conduct a carefully crafted capital campaign
- Optimize your current fundraising work
- Build a community of lifelong partners
- And more!

LEARN MORE AT THEFOCUSGROUP.COM

the
FOCUSgroup
taking donors seriously®

Exclusive Insights to Transform Your Fundraising

Discover revolutionary principles and fundraising practices from *Turning Donors into Partners* in a video course featuring author and fundraising expert Brad Layland.

With simplicity, clarity, wisdom, and humor, Brad shares inspiring stories and delivers actionable principles, equipping you to transform your fundraising into a life-giving, energizing experience.

Build a generous community of partners and step into the work God has given you to do.

To start watching now, visit

LEARN.DONORSINTOPARTNERS.COM